Making Sense

A Student's Guide to Research and Writing

Eighth Edition

Making Sense

A Student's Guide to Research and Writing

Margot Northey
Joan McKibbin

OXFORD
UNIVERSITY PRESS

OXFORD
UNIVERSITY PRESS

Oxford University Press is a department of the University of Oxford.
It furthers the University's objective of excellence in research, scholarship,
and education by publishing worldwide. Oxford is a registered trade mark of
Oxford University Press in the UK and in certain other countries.

Published in Canada by
Oxford University Press
8 Sampson Mews, Suite 204,
Don Mills, Ontario M3C 0H5 Canada

www.oupcanada.com

First Edition published in 1983
Second Edition published in 1987
Third Edition published in 1993
Fourth Edition published in 2002
Fifth edition published in 2007
Sixth edition published in 2009
Seventh edition published in 2012

Library and Archives Canada Cataloguing in Publication
Northey, Margot, 1940-, author
Making sense : a student's guide to research and writing / Margot
Northey, Joan McKibbin. -- Eighth edition.

(The making sense series)
Includes bibliographical references and index.
ISBN 978-0-19-901016-5 (pbk.)

1. Report writing. 2. English language--Rhetoric. 3. Exposition
(Rhetoric). I. McKibbin, Joan, author II. Title. III. Series: Making
sense series

LB2369.N67 2015   808'.042   C2015-900046-7

Cover images: (clockwise from top left) © iStock/TommL; © iStock/Jasmina007; © iStock/syolacan

Oxford University Press is committed to our environment.
This book is printed on Forest Stewardship Council® certified paper
and comes from responsible sources.

Printed and bound in Canada

1 2 3 4 — 18 17 16 15

Contents

A Note to the Student   *vi*
Acknowledgements   *vii*

1.   Writing and Thinking   1
2.   Writing an Essay   8
3.   Writing a Book Report   39
4.   Writing a Lab Report   45
5.   Writing a Business Report   54
6.   Using Illustrations   68
7.   Documenting Sources   73
8.   Giving an Oral Presentation   110
9.   Writing Examinations   119
10.   Writing a Resumé and Letter of Application   128
11.   Writing with Style   137
12.   Common Errors in Grammar and Usage   153
13.   Punctuation   167
14.   Misused Words and Phrases   183

Glossary   *198*
Index   *205*

A Note to the Student

By now, most students are comfortable using computers in their studies and understand their benefits in preparing written and spoken material. However, the truth remains that the effectiveness of communication has less to do with technology than with content and how it is presented. The common saying "Garbage in, garbage out" underscores that nothing will compensate for poor information. Yet relevant information by itself will not bring you success with essays, reports, or presentations. How clearly you organize and express your ideas matters just as much. It's a challenge that *Making Sense* will help you meet.

Writing in university or college is not fundamentally different from writing elsewhere. Yet each piece of writing has its own special purposes, and these are what determine its shape and tone. This edition of *Making Sense* examines both the general precepts for effective writing and the special requirements of academic work (especially the essay and the report); it also points out some of the most common errors in student composition and suggests how to avoid or correct them. Written mostly in the form of guidelines rather than strict rules—since few rules are inviolable—this book should help you escape the common pitfalls of student writing and develop confidence through an understanding of basic principles and a mastery of sound techniques.

Good writing does not come naturally; even for the best writers it's mostly hard work. Even though computers and technology have simplified the mechanics of writing, the completed assignment usually reflects the old formula: 10 per cent inspiration and 90 per cent perspiration.

This eighth edition of *Making Sense* includes

- new material on how to argue a case, especially with a controversial subject;
- revised and updated discussions of the possibilities and potential drawbacks of various technologies available to students; and
- new guidelines for online applications for employment or graduate school.

As always, the intent of *Making Sense* is to give you a clear, concise, and readable guide that will accompany you throughout your academic career.

Acknowledgements

Many thanks to our reviewers: Krista Kesselring of Dalhousie University, Reyes Bertolin Cebrian of the University of Calgary, and Sherry Johnson of York University. We would also like to thank our editors at Oxford University Press, notably Tamara Capar and Dana Hopkins, for their expertise and hard work.

Writing and Thinking

1

> **In this chapter, we will examine**
> - writing for a specific purpose and audience;
> - strategies for creating an appropriate tone; and
> - using culturally sensitive language.

Introduction

You are not likely to produce clear writing unless you have first done some clear thinking, and thinking can't be hurried. It follows that the most important step you can take is to leave yourself enough time to think. Psychologists have shown that you can't always solve a difficult problem by "putting your mind to it"—by determined reasoning alone. Sometimes when you're stuck it's best to take a break, sleep on it, and let the subconscious or creative part of your brain take over for a while. Very often a period of relaxation will produce a new approach or solution. Just remember that leaving time for creative reflection isn't the same thing as sitting around listening to music until inspiration strikes out of the blue.

Initial Strategies

Writing is about making choices: choices about what ideas you want to present and how you want to present them. With practice, making decisions becomes easier, but no matter how fluent you become, with each piece of writing you will still have to choose.

You can narrow the field of choice from the start if you realize that you are not writing for just anybody, anywhere, for no particular reason. With any writing you do, it's always a sound strategy to ask yourself two basic questions:

- What is the purpose of this piece of writing?
- Who is the reader?

Your first reaction may be, "Well, I'm writing for my instructor to satisfy a course requirement," but that's not specific enough. To be useful, your answers have to be precise.

Think about the purpose

Depending on the assignment, your purpose in writing an essay may be any one (or more) of the following:

- to show your knowledge of a topic or text;
- to show that you understand certain terms or theories;
- to show that you can do independent research;
- to show that you can apply a specific theory to new material;
- to demonstrate your ability to evaluate secondary sources;
- to show that you can think critically or creatively.

An assignment designed to see if you have read and understood specific material requires a different approach from one that's meant to test your critical thinking. In the first case, your approach will tend to be expository, with the emphasis on presenting facts. In the second case, you will probably want to structure your essay around a particular argument or assertion that other people might dispute. Your aim in this kind of argumentative or persuasive essay is to bring your reader around to your point of view. (Argumentative essays are discussed in greater detail in Chapter 2.)

Think about the reader

Thinking about the reader does not mean playing up to the instructor. To convince a particular person that your own views are sound you have to consider his or her way of thinking. Imagine that you are writing a paper on the effects of terrorism for a sociology professor. Your analysis will be different than it would be if you were writing for an economics or history professor. You will have to make specific decisions about the terms you should explain, the background information you should supply, and the details you will need in order to convince that particular reader. In the same way, if you plan to write a paper defending tax credits for families paying private school tuition and your reader is a big supporter of public education, you will have to anticipate any arguments that he or she may raise so that you can address them. If you don't know who will be reading your paper—your professor, your tutorial leader, or a marker—just imagine someone intelligent, knowledgeable, and interested, skeptical enough to question your ideas but flexible enough to adopt them if your evidence is convincing.

Think about the length

Before you start writing, you will also need to think about the length of your assignment in relation to the time you can spend on it. If both the topic and the length are prescribed, it should be fairly easy for you to assess the level of detail required and the amount of research you will need to do. If only the length is prescribed, that restriction will help you decide how broad or how narrow a topic you should choose (see pages 15–17). You should also keep in mind how much the assignment is worth. A paper that is worth 50 per cent of your final grade will merit more of your time and effort than one that is worth only 10 per cent.

Think about the tone

In everyday writing to friends, such as in e-mails and texts, you probably adopt a casual tone, but academic writing is usually more formal. Just how formal you need to be will depend on the kind of assignment and the instructions you have been given. In some cases—for example, if your psychology professor asks you to describe certain personal experiences in a journal—you may be able to use an informal style. Essays and reports, however, usually require a more formal tone. What kind of style is too informal for most academic work? Here are the main signs:

Use of slang

Although the occasional slang word or phrase may be useful for special effect, frequent use of slang is not acceptable in academic writing because slang expressions are usually regional and short-lived. They may mean different things to different groups at different times. (Just think of how widely the meanings of *hot*, *cool*, and *sick* can vary, depending on the circumstances.) In a formal essay, where clarity of expression is important, it's better to use words with well-established meanings that will be understood by the greatest number of readers.

Excessive use of first-person pronouns

Since a formal essay is not a personal outpouring, you want to keep it from becoming *I*-centred. There is no need to begin every sentence with "I think" or "In my view" when the facts or arguments speak for themselves. It's certainly acceptable to use the occasional first-person pronoun if the assignment calls for your point of view—as long as your opinions are backed by evidence. Also, if the choice is between using *I* and creating a tangle of passive constructions (for example, "It is hoped that it can reasonably be concluded, based on the evidence that has been presented, that . . ."), it's almost always better to choose *I*. (A hint: when you do use *I*, it will be less noticeable if you place it in the middle of the sentence rather than at the beginning—a point that is especially useful when writing resumés as well as essays.) Here are some examples of ways to avoid both *I*-centred and unnecessarily passive sentences:

- ✗ Having analyzed the new legislation, I believe it is flawed.

- ✗ The new legislation, having been analyzed, appears to me to be flawed.

- ✓ When analyzed, the new legislation seems flawed.

- ✗ In this essay, Atwood's portrayal of wilderness will be investigated, and the repeated conflict between wilderness and civilization will be discussed.

- ✓ **[better]** In this essay, I will investigate Atwood's portrayal of nature and discuss the repeated conflict between wilderness and civilization.

- ✓ **[best]** This essay will investigate Atwood's portrayal of nature and discuss the repeated conflict between nature and civilization.

Frequent use of contractions

Generally speaking, contractions such as *can't* and *isn't* are not suitable for academic writing, although they may be fine for letters or other informal kinds of writing—for example, this handbook. This is not to say that you should avoid using contractions altogether; even the most serious academic writing can sound stilted or unnatural without any contractions at all. Just be sure that when you use contractions in a college or university essay you use them sparingly, since excessive use of contractions makes formal writing sound chatty and informal.

Finding a suitable tone for academic writing can be a challenge. The problem with trying to avoid excessive informality is that you may be tempted to go to the other extreme. If your writing sounds stiff or pompous, you may be using too many inflated phrases, long words, or passive constructions (see Chapter 11). When in doubt, remember that a more formal style is the best option.

Guidelines for Writing

Whenever you embark on a writing project, try to keep the following guidelines in mind:

- Think about your audience, the reader or readers of your writing.
- Be clear about your subject and your purpose, what it is you hope to achieve.
- Define your terms.
- Include only relevant material; don't pad your writing to achieve a certain number of words.
- Strive for consistency of expression throughout the work.
- Make sure you are accurate in all of your statements, in your analysis and presentation of data, and in your documentation of sources.
- Order your information logically.
- Be simple and clear in expressing your ideas.
- Make sure that your argument is coherent.
- Draw conclusions that are clearly based on your evidence.
- Allow yourself lots of time to work on drafts before completing the final copy.
- Make sure to edit and proofread your work carefully.

In the chapters that follow, we will consider these guidelines in greater detail.

Using Culturally Sensitive Language

As concern with political correctness grows, we need to pay more attention to perceived offence in the language we use—both spoken and written. Just as you give thought to your reader(s) and to the kind of tone you wish to create, you will also want to use language that avoids demeaning anyone unnecessarily and that is free of terms that have a derogatory connotation. This does not mean that you should not express a strong opinion. Nor does it mean you should resort to euphemism or roundabout language, such as saying "economically disadvantaged" when you mean "poor." It does mean being sensitive, especially in areas of gender, religion, race, and culture.

Gender

One of the most common problems in writing today is that of perceived gender bias, since unfortunately the English language does not have a neutral, singular pronoun referring to both a man and a woman. At one time, it would have been acceptable to refer to a person of either sex as "he":

> If an employee becomes redundant, he will receive a severance package.

This practice is still preferred by many traditionalists and stylists. They see "he" as both a specific gender and a generic term similar to nouns like "mankind" or "humanity." But as sensitivity to bias has increased, we have become more careful about the use of a generic pronoun. Here are some options for avoiding the problem:

- Use the passive voice:

> A severance package will be given to an employee who becomes redundant.

However, since passive verbs sap the energy of prose, use them sparingly.

- Restructure the sentence:

> An employee who becomes redundant will receive a severance package.

- Use "he or she," although this is cumbersome and may annoy some readers:

> If an employee becomes redundant, he or she will receive a severance package.

- Use the plural form:

> If employees become redundant, they will receive severance
> packages.

Another option is to alternate, using the masculine form in one instance and the feminine form in the next.

Recently, some writers have used the neutral "they" to refer to a singular antecedent:

> When a writer aims for simplicity, they will occasionally break with
> grammatical convention.

Be careful, however. This approach may still raise the hackles of a traditional reader.

Another trouble spot involves gender-specific nouns, such as *stewardess*, *waitress*, and *fireman*. The solution in these cases is to look for gender-free words, for example, *flight attendant*, *server*, and *firefighter*.

Race and culture

The names used to describe someone's racial or cultural identity often carry negative connotations for some readers although they have been widely used and accepted in the past. For example, consider the term *Negro*. The search for neutral language has produced alternatives such as *Black* or *African Canadian*. We have similar problems with the term *Indian*, with alternatives such as *Aboriginal*, *Native*, and *First Nations*. The best approach is to find out what the racial or cultural group in question prefers. Even if there isn't an easy answer, being aware of a potential problem is already part of the solution.

There are many other areas where the effort to develop and use neutral language has made an impact. To be politically correct, writers usually refer not to *old people* but to *seniors*, and to someone as *challenged* or having *special needs* rather than being *handicapped*. Occasionally, the search for inoffensive language leads to ever-changing terms or vague euphemisms, such as when *garbage man* became *waste collector* and then *sanitation engineer*. Whatever the situation, be sensitive to the power of the words you use, and take the time to search for language that is unbiased but not cumbersome.

Writing an Essay

Introduction

If you are one of the many students who dread writing academic essays, you will find that following a few simple steps in planning and organizing will make the task easier—and the result better.

This is not a one-size-fits-all process, and the amount of time you spend on each stage will depend on the nature of the assignment. For a short, straightforward essay requiring little research, you will likely spend most of the time drafting and editing. For a more complex essay, when you must take into account what others before you have said, it's likely that over half of your time will be spent on research and planning. Understanding the total process of completing a written assignment will serve you well, whether you are a first-year undergraduate or a post-graduate student.

The Planning Stage

Some students claim they can write essays without any planning at all. On the rare occasions when they succeed, their writing is usually not as spontaneous as they might think; they have actually thought or talked a good deal about the subject in advance and have come to the task with some ready-made ideas. More often, students who try to write a lengthy essay without planning just end up frustrated. They get stuck in the middle and don't know how to finish, or they suddenly realize that they're rambling.

In contrast, most writers say that the planning stage is the most important part of the whole process. Certainly the evidence shows that poor planning usually leads to disorganized writing. In the majority of students' essays, the single greatest improvement would be not better research or better grammar but better organization.

This insistence on planning doesn't rule out exploratory writing (see page 22). Many people find that the act of writing itself is the best way to generate ideas or to overcome writer's block; the hard decisions about organization come after they've put something down on the page. You can organize before or after you begin to write; however, at some point you need to plan.

Read primary material

Primary material is the direct evidence—usually books or articles—on which you will base your essay. Surprising as it may seem, the best way to begin working with this material is to give it a fast initial skim. Don't just start reading from beginning to end; first look at the table of contents, scan the index, and read the preface or introduction to get a sense of the author's purpose and plan. Getting an overview will allow you to focus your questions for a more purposeful and analytic second reading. Make no mistake: a superficial reading is not all you need. You still have to work through the material carefully a second time. But an initial skim followed by a focused second reading will give you a much more thorough understanding than one slow plod ever will.

A warning about secondary sources

Always be sure you have a firm grasp of the primary material before you turn to secondary sources (analyses of the primary material). Instructors in some disciplines discourage secondary reading in introductory courses. They know that students who turn to commentaries may be so overwhelmed by the weight of authority that they will rely too heavily on them.

In some instances—and especially in the sciences—students are encouraged to review recent literature on the topic they have chosen to see where their views stand in relation to those of the experts in the field. However, if you turn to commentaries as a way around the difficulty of understanding the primary source, or if you base your argument solely on the interpretations of others, you may end up producing a trite, second-hand essay. Your interpretation could even be downright wrong, because at this stage you might not know enough about a subject to be able to evaluate the commentary. Secondary sources are an important part of learning and are essential to many research papers, but they can never substitute for your own active reading of the primary material.

Analyze your subject

Whether the subject you start with is one that has been assigned or suggested by your instructor or is one that you have chosen yourself, it is bound to be too broad for an essay topic. You will have to analyze your subject in order to find a way of limiting it.

Ask questions

The best way of analyzing is to ask questions that will lead to useful answers. How do you form that kind of question? Journalists approach their stories through a six-question formula: who? what? where? when? why? and how? For example, starting with the question what? and applying it to a work of literature, you might ask: "What contrasts of character are there?"; "What role do the minor characters play?"; "What are the good or evil qualities of the characters?" How and why questions are often the most productive, since they take you beyond information gathering and force you to analyze and interpret. For example: "How does the author portray women (or old age, or Aboriginal people)?"

To take another subject, consider some of the same kinds of questions you could ask about Canada and free trade:

- What are the economic advantages of Canada's participation in free trade with the US and Mexico? What are the economic disadvantages?
- Who in Canada has benefited the most from the North American Free Trade Agreement?
- Who are the main opponents of NAFTA? Why do they oppose it?
- Why are there still trade disputes between Canada and the US in spite of NAFTA?
- How are Canadian women affected by free trade? How does their experience compare with that of women in Mexico and the US?

Most often, the questions you ask initially—and the answers to them—will be general, but they will stimulate more specific questions that will help you refine your topic and develop a thesis statement.

Try the three-C approach

A more systematic scheme for analyzing a subject is the three-C approach. It forces you to look at a subject from three different perspectives, asking basic questions about components, change, and context:

Components:
- What parts or categories can the subject be broken down into?
- Can the main divisions be subdivided?

Change:
- What features have changed?
- Is there a trend?
- What caused the change?
- What are the results of the change?

Context:
- What is the larger issue surrounding the subject?
- In what tradition or school of thought does the subject belong?
- How is the subject similar to, and different from, related subjects?

What are the **components** *of the subject?*

In other words, how might the subject be broken down into smaller elements? This question forces you to take a close look at the subject and helps you avoid oversimplification or easy generalization.

Suppose that your assignment is to discuss the policies of William Lyon Mackenzie King. After asking yourself about components, you might decide that you can split the subject into (1) domestic policies and (2) foreign policies. Alternatively, you might divide it into (1) economic policies, (2) political policies, and (3) social policies. Then, since these components are too broad, you might break them down further, splitting economic policies into (a) fiscal and (b) monetary policies, separating political policies into (a) relations with the provinces and (b) relations with other countries, and subdividing social policies according to the different social groups targeted.

Similarly, if you were analyzing the imagery in one of Shakespeare's plays, you could ask, "What are the different types?" (for example, similes, metaphors, and allusions). Or, "What are the content groupings?" (for instance, animal images, solar images, and military images). If you were writing a sociology essay on juvenile crime, you could ask, "What are the different types and frequencies of juvenile crime? Do crimes differ among juveniles of different sexes and ages?"

Approaching your subject this way will help you appreciate its complexity and avoid making sweeping generalizations that don't apply to all areas of the subject. In addition, asking questions about the components of your subject may help you find one aspect of it that is not too large for you to explore in detail.

What features of the subject suggest change?

This question helps you to think about trends. It can also point to antecedents or causes of an occurrence as well as to the likely results or implications of a change.

Suppose you have decided to focus on Mackenzie King's economic policies. You might consider whether those policies shifted over a period of years. Did he express contradictory views in different documents? What caused changes in a specific policy? What were the effects of these changes?

For the essay on Shakespeare's imagery you could ask whether a pattern of repeated images emerges as the drama proceeds. Does a particular image change in its use or connotation? What is the effect of the change? What might be the reason for it?

On the subject of juvenile crime you might ask, "Have there been changes or trends in the rate of criminal offences committed?" or "Have there been changes in the nature or definition of delinquency?" Then ask, "What are the causes or results of these changes?"

What is the context of the subject?

What particular school of thought or tradition does the subject belong to? What are the similarities and differences between this subject and related ones? The following are typical context questions:

- How do Mackenzie King's trade policies compare with those of Paul Martin and other Liberal prime ministers? How do they compare with the policies of Stephen Harper or other Conservative prime ministers?
- How does the use of imagery (either general or of a particular type) in play X differ from that in the earlier play Y? How does Shakespeare's use of a specific type of imagery compare with, say, Marlowe's?
- How does the rate or nature of juvenile delinquency in Canada compare with that in Australia or Britain? Or with the rate and nature of adult crimes?

General as most of these questions are, you will find that they stimulate more specific questions—and thoughts—about the material from which you can choose your topic and decide on your controlling idea. Remember that the ability to ask intelligent questions is one of the most important, though often underrated, skills that you can develop for any work, in university and elsewhere.[1]

Analyze a prescribed topic

Even if the topic of your essay is supplied by your instructor, you still need to analyze it carefully. Try underlining key words to make sure that you don't neglect anything. Distinguish the main focus from subordinate concerns. A common error in dealing with prescribed topics is to emphasize one portion while overlooking or minimizing another. Give each part its proper due, and make sure that you actually do what the instructions tell you to do. For example, consider the instructions implicit in these verbs:

outline	State simply, without much development of each point (unless asked).
trace	Review by looking back—on stages or steps in a process, or on causes of an occurrence.
explain	Show how or why something happens.
discuss	Examine or analyze in an orderly way. This instruction allows you considerable freedom, as long as you take into account contrary evidence or ideas.
compare	Examine differences as well as similarities. (For a more detailed discussion, see pages 24–5.)
evaluate	Analyze strengths and weaknesses, providing an overall assessment of worth.

These and other verbs tell you how to approach the topic; don't confuse them.

Develop a thesis

As Chapter 1 explains, not all essays centre on arguments. Yet every essay, even the expository kind, needs a controlling idea around which all the material can be organized. This central idea is usually known as a thesis, though in the case of an expository essay you may prefer to think of it as a theme. Consider these statements:

> THEME: Each of Canada's provinces and territories faces a unique set of regional challenges.
>
> THESIS: Canada would be better governed if there were fewer provinces and territories.

The first is a straightforward statement of fact; an essay centred on such a theme would probably focus on simply describing those different regional challenges. By contrast, the second statement is one with which other people might well disagree; an essay based on this thesis would have to present a convincing argument. The expository form can produce an informative and interesting essay, but many students prefer the argumentative approach because it's easier to organize and is more likely to produce strong writing.

If you have decided to present an argument, you will probably want to create a working thesis as the focal point around which you can start organizing your material. This working thesis doesn't have to be final: you are free to change it at any stage in your planning. It simply serves as a linchpin, holding together your information and ideas as you organize. It will help you define your intentions, make your research more selective, and focus your essay.

At some point in the writing process you will probably want to make your working thesis into an explicit thesis statement that can appear in your introduction. This is not always necessary: as you gain experience, you may choose to put your thesis later or just imply it rather than stating it. Even if you don't intend to include it in your final draft, though, you need to know what your thesis statement is and to keep it in mind throughout the writing process. It's worth taking the time to work this statement out carefully. Use a complete sentence to express it, and above all make sure that it is restricted, unified, and precise.[2]

Restrict your thesis

A restricted thesis is one that is narrow enough for you to examine thoroughly in the space you have available. Suppose, for example, that your general subject is the New Democratic Party. Such a subject is much too broad to be handled properly in an essay of one or two thousand words; you must restrict it in some way and create a line of argument for which you can supply adequate supporting evidence. Following the analytic questioning process, you might find that you want to restrict it by time: "Following the 2011 federal election, the NDP assumed a radically different role in Canadian Parliament." Or you might prefer to limit it by geography: "Socialized medicine in Saskatchewan was a natural outgrowth of local culture."

To take an example from literature, suppose that your general subject for a two-thousand-word essay is the work of Hugh MacLennan. You might want to limit your essay by discussing a prominent theme in one or two novels: "Although MacLennan exposes the dark side of religion in *Each Man's Son*, he also reveals a yearning for spiritual wholeness." Or you could focus on some aspect of characterization: "In *Each Man's Son* and *The Watch That Ends the Night*, MacLennan creates drama through his contrast of character types." Whatever the discipline or subject, make sure that your topic is restricted enough that you can explore it in depth.

Create a unified thesis

A unified thesis must have one controlling idea. Beware of the double-headed thesis: "Brian Mulroney introduced some of the boldest economic policies in Canadian history, but his failure to bring Quebec into the Constitution led to his downfall." What is the controlling idea here? The boldness of Mulroney's economic policies or the reason for his downfall? It's possible to have two or more related ideas in a thesis, but only if one of them is clearly in control, with all the other ideas subordinated to it: "Although Brian Mulroney was widely applauded for his efforts to bring Quebec into the Constitution, his eventual failure to do so was the cause of his political downfall."

Create a precise thesis

A precise thesis should not contain vague terms such as *interesting* and *significant*, as in "Mustafa Kemal Atatürk, the founder of the Turkish Republic, was one of the most interesting heads of state of the twentieth century." Does *interesting* mean "effective or daring in his policies," "controversial," or "intriguing"? Don't say simply, "Sheila Watson's use of symbols is an important feature of her writing" when you can be more precise about the work you are discussing, the kind of symbols you've found there, and exactly what they do: "In *The Double Hook*, Sheila Watson adapts traditional symbols from Christian and Indian mythology to underscore the theme of spiritual death and regeneration."

Remember to be as specific as possible when creating a thesis in order to focus your essay. Don't just make an assertion—give the main reason for it. Instead of saying, "Many Westerners are resentful of central Canada" and leaving it at that, add an explanation: ". . . because of historic grievances such as tariffs, freight rates, and the national energy policy." If these details make your thesis sound awkward, don't worry; a working thesis is only a planning device, something to guide the organization of your ideas. You can change the wording in your final essay.

Research your topic

If your topic requires more facts or evidence than the primary material provides, or if you want to know other people's opinions on the subject, you will need to do some research. Some students like to read around in the subject area before they decide on an essay topic; for them, the thesis comes after the exploration. You may find this approach useful for some essays, but generally it's better to narrow your scope and plan a tentative thesis before you turn to secondary sources—you'll save time and produce a more original essay.

Explore library resources

Libraries used to be places where students went for books or paper articles. Now students increasingly go to libraries for help with online research. Of course you can conduct much online research on your own, but the trick is to find the most reliable sources from the range of possibilities. Librarians can be a tremendous help in pointing you in the right direction. They are the best first resource. They will be glad to show you not only the materials available at the library but also the wealth of online sources you can access from your home computer, without going back to the library. Two of the most useful resources available through the library are online catalogues and electronic databases.

Online catalogues provide remote access to a list of all the holdings at your library, including books, videos, and print journals. A search by keyword will give you a list of relevant sources in your library and possibly in other libraries as well. Interlibrary loan services enable you to access these off-campus resources quickly at little or no cost.

Electronic databases simplify your search for information because they make millions of journal articles available from a single source. Libraries subscribe to online services such as JSTOR, ProQuest, or EBSCOhost which index a subset of smaller databases, thereby acting as gateways to a huge network of online journals. A single search gives you access to articles in thousands of different journals.

To conduct a database search from a remote computer, simply go to your library website and follow the link to the database of your choice. You can then search by subject, author, or title. In addition, there are usually options for narrowing the search if you prefer, for example by restricting it to specific journals or disciplines.

Your search results will provide you with a list of articles on your subject, some of which are available in full text, allowing you to read the material online as well as save, print, or e-mail it. Most databases also have a Cite feature, which shows you how to format the article correctly in a bibliography.

Search the Web

You are no doubt accustomed to using the Web and can find information on just about anything using your favourite search engines. Although online information can be immediate and current, you need to be wary, since the Web spreads much that is unreliable. Information is often based on half-truths—or is plain false.

Tips for evaluating online sources

Unlike academic journals, which are peer reviewed and tend to be reliable sources of information, many websites do not have editorial boards. They publish material that has not undergone any review process. Remember that anyone can publish online, as the proliferation of blogs will attest. You want to be sure that the author or publisher of any material you use has the necessary authority to lend credibility to the site.

Although not foolproof, these guidelines will help you avoid research bloopers:

- **Pay attention to domain names.** These are identification strings which identify the source or publisher of the website. Every domain name ends with a TLD—top-level domain—which can give you an indication of possible bias. Examples of TLDs are *.gc.ca* for the Canadian government or *.edu* for educational institutions in the US. There may be additional clues in the URLs of some sites. For example, a tilde (~) indicates a personal page where you are likely to find expressions of opinion.
- **Look for information about the site host.** You should be able to find a statement on the home page identifying the host, listing contact information, and giving details about the credentials of any contributors to the site.
- **Determine the currency of the site.** There should be a clear indication of when the material was written, published, and last revised.

- **Evaluate the accuracy of the information.** Be sure to check facts and figures with other sources. Data published on the site should be documented in citations or a bibliography, and research methods should be explained.
- **Avoid wikis.** These are collaborative websites that allow anyone to contribute or modify content. A free encyclopedia that anyone can edit may be a quick and easy way of finding something out, but it's not the kind of sound research on which you want to base your essay. Although editors may continually check the veracity of contributions to the site, there is no guarantee that what you are reading is accurate.
- **Be wary of blogs.** Although some companies have official blogs that can offer good advice about subjects like the stock market and real estate, many are simply online diaries published by a rapidly increasing number of people who are expressing personal opinion and nothing more. Using such unverified material can seriously undermine your essay, as many a student has discovered.
- **Assess the overall quality of the site.** A major clue to the reliability of the website is its level of correctness and standard of writing. Typos and grammatical errors are clear indications of unprofessional work that has not been monitored for correctness and accuracy. A website author who doesn't pay attention to these details probably doesn't have fastidious research methods either.

Make clear notes

Finding your research material is one thing; taking notes that are dependable and easy to use is another. Here are some guidelines for taking good notes:

- For every entry, check that the bibliographic details are complete, including the name of the author, the title of the source, the publisher, the place and date of publication, and the page number. For an online source, record the URL, website name, date of publication, and date of access. Nothing is more frustrating than using a piece of information in an essay only to find that you aren't sure where it came from. Record the bibliographic details in the citation format you plan to use for your paper; that way, when you're preparing your list of references later on, you can copy the source directly. (You will find detailed information about citation formats in Chapter 7.)
- Check that quotations are copied precisely, and, since you may end up using only part of the quotation, be sure to mark any page breaks.

- Include page numbers for every reference, even if you paraphrase or summarize the idea rather than copying it word for word.

Create an outline

Individual writers differ in their need for a formal plan. Some say they never have an outline, while others maintain they can't write without one; most fall somewhere in between. Since organization is such a common problem, though, it's a good idea to know how to draw up an effective plan. Of course, the exact form your outline takes will depend on the pattern you use to develop your ideas—whether you are defining, classifying, comparing, or arguing, for example (see pages 23–7).

If you tend to have problems organizing your writing, your outline should be formal and in complete sentences. On the other hand, if your mind is naturally logical, you may find it's enough just to jot down a few words on a scrap of paper. For most students, an informal but well-organized outline in point form is the most useful model. The following is an example of an outline for an argumentative essay:

THESIS: When Prime Minster Pierre Elliott Trudeau first came to power, his style was seen as an enormous asset, but by the '80s the same style was increasingly seen as a liability.

I. Trudeau's early style perceived in positive light
    A. Charismatic
        1. Public adulation: "Trudeaumania"
        2. Media awe
    B. Intellectual
    C. Tough
        1. Handling of journalists
        2. Handling of Quebec
    D. Anti-establishment
        1. Swinging lifestyle
        2. Disregard for government traditions

II. Later reversal: Trudeau's image becomes negative
    A. Irritating
        1. Public opinion polls
        2. Media disenchantment

  B. Out of touch with economic reality
   1. National Energy Program
   2. National debt
   3. Budgetary deficit
  C. Confrontational
   1. With individual dissenters
   2. With premiers
   3. With Opposition leaders
  D. Arrogant
   1. Extravagant lifestyle in time of recession
   2. Autocratic approach to governing
 Conclusion

The following example shows an outline for an expository essay with a more descriptive theme:

THEME: Because of their importance for survival, refined navigational skills are found throughout the animal kingdom. These skills are based on a wide variety of different cues.

 I. Orienting and navigating seen in many different kinds of animals
  A. Birds
   1. Arctic tern
   2. Homing pigeon
  B. Insects
   1. Army ant
   2. Monarch butterfly
  C. Fish
   1. Salmon
   2. Eels
   3. Tuna

 II. Navigating serves different purposes
  A. Migration
   1. Favourable climate
    a) Going south
    b) Going north
   2. Food availability
   3. Breeding grounds

    B. Locating local food sources
       1. Honeybee
       2. Ant

III. Navigating animals use different cues
    A. Celestial cues
       1. Sun compass
       2. Star navigation
    B. Terrestrial cues
       1. Geomagnetism
       2. Barometric pressure
       3. Odour trails
       4. Landmarks
Conclusion

The guidelines for both types of outline are simple:

- **Code your categories.** Use different sets of markings to establish the relative importance of your entries. The example here moves from Roman numerals to uppercase letters to Arabic numerals to lowercase letters, but you could use another system. The software you use will likely have a default format but also offer alternatives.
- **Categorize according to importance.** Make sure that only items of equal value are put in equivalent categories. Give major points more weight than minor ones.
- **Check lines of connection.** Make sure that each of the main categories is directly linked to the central thesis; then see that each subcategory is directly linked to the larger category that contains it. Checking these lines of connection is the best way of preventing essay muddle.
- **Be consistent.** In arranging your points, use the same order every time. You may choose to move from the most important point to the least important, or vice versa, as long as you are consistent.
- **Be logical.** In addition to checking for lines of connection and organizational consistency, make sure that the overall development of your work is logical. Does each heading/idea/discussion flow into the next, leading your reader through the material in the most logical manner?
- **Use parallel wording.** Phrasing each entry in a similar way makes it easier for your reader to follow your line of thinking. For a discussion of parallel structure, see page 166.

Be prepared to change your outline at any time in the writing process. Your initial outline is not meant to put an iron clamp on your thinking but to relieve anxiety about where you're heading. A careful outline prevents frustration and dead ends—that "I'm stuck. Where do I go from here?" feeling. But since the very act of writing will usually generate new ideas, you should be ready to modify your original plan. Just remember that any new outline must have the consistency and clear connections required for a unified essay.

The Writing Stage

Writing the first draft

Rather than striving for perfection from the moment they begin to write, most writers find it easier to compose the first draft as quickly as possible and do extensive revisions later. However you begin, you can't expect the first draft to be the final copy. Skilled writers know that revising is a necessary part of the writing process and that the care taken with revisions makes the difference between a mediocre essay and a good one.

Many writers face writer's block. If you are one of them, remember that you don't need to write all parts of the essay in the same order as they are to appear in the final copy. In fact, many students find the introduction the hardest part to write. If you face the first blank page with a growing sense of paralysis, try leaving the introduction until later and start with the first idea in your outline. If you feel so intimidated that you haven't even been able to draw up an outline, you might try the approach suggested by John Trimble and begin anywhere: just write, "Well, it seems to me that . . ." and begin talking onscreen (or on paper).[3] Instead of picking just the right study music or running out for a snack, just try to get going. Don't worry about grammar or wording; at this stage, the object is to get your writing juices flowing.

Of course, you can't expect this kind of exploratory writing to resemble the first draft that follows an outline. You will probably need to do a great deal more changing and reorganizing, but at least you will have the relief of seeing words on a page. Many experienced writers—and not only those with writer's block—consider this the most productive way to proceed.

Developing your ideas: Some common patterns

The way you develop your ideas will depend on your essay topic, and topics can vary enormously. Even so, most essays follow one or another of a handful of basic organizational patterns. Here are some of the patterns, along with suggestions for using them effectively.

Defining

Sometimes a whole essay is an extended definition, explaining the meaning of a term that is complicated, controversial, or simply important to your field of study, for example, nationalism in political science, monetarism in economics, or existentialism in philosophy. Rather than making your whole paper an extended definition, you may decide just to begin your paper by defining a key term before shifting to a different organizational pattern. In either case, make your definition exact; it should be broad enough to include all the things that belong in the category but narrow enough to exclude things that don't belong. A good definition builds a kind of verbal fence around a word, herding together all the members of the class and cutting off all outsiders.

For any discussion of a term that goes beyond a bare definition, you should give concrete illustrations or examples. Depending on the nature of your essay, these could vary in length from one or two sentences to several paragraphs or even pages. If you are defining monetarism, for instance, you will probably want to discuss at some length the theories of leading monetarists.

In an extended definition, it's also useful to point out the differences between the term you're defining and any others that may be related to or confused with it. For instance, if you are defining pathos, you might want to distinguish it from tragedy; if you are defining deviance, you might want to distinguish it from criminality; if you are defining common law, you might want to distinguish it from statute law.

Classifying

Classifying means dividing something into its separate parts according to a given principle of selection. The principle or criterion may vary. You could classify crops, for example, according to how they grow (above the ground or below the ground), how long they take to mature, or what climatic conditions they require; or you could classify members of a given population according to age, occupation, income, race, religion, or gender. If you are organizing your essay by a system of classification, remember the following:

- All members of a class must be accounted for. If any are left over, you need to alter or add some categories.

- Categories can be divided into subcategories. You should consider using subcategories if there are significant differences within a category. If, for instance, you are classifying the workforce according to occupation, you might want to create subcategories according to income level.
- Any subcategory should contain at least two items.

Explaining a process

This kind of organization shows how something works or has worked, whether it is the weather cycle, the justice system, or the stages in a political or military campaign. You need to be systematic, to break down the process into a series of steps or stages. Although your order will vary, most often it will be chronological, in which case you should see that the sequence is accurate and easy to follow. Whatever the arrangement, you can generally make the process clearer if you start a new paragraph for each new stage.

Tracing causes or effects

A cause-or-effect analysis is really a particular kind of process discussion, in which certain events are shown to have led to or resulted from other events. Usually, you are explaining why something happened. The main warning here is to avoid oversimplifying. If you are tracing causes, distinguish between a direct cause and a contributing cause, between what is a condition of something happening and what is merely a correlation or coincidence. For example, if you discover that both the age of the average driver in Canada and the number of accidents caused by drunk drivers are increasing, you cannot jump to the conclusion that older drivers are the cause of the increase in drunk-driving accidents. Similarly, you must be sure that the result you identify is a genuine product of the event or action.

Comparing

Students sometimes forget that comparing things means showing differences as well as similarities—even if the instructions do not say "compare and contrast." Suppose, for instance, that you were comparing negative and positive opinions on the effects of free trade in various sectors. The easiest method for comparison—though not always the best—is to discuss the first subject in the comparison thoroughly and then move on to the second:

```
positive views:    resources
                   manufacturing
                   culture


negative views:    resources
                   manufacturing
                   culture
```

The problem with this kind of comparison is that it often sounds like two separate essays slapped together.

To be successful you must integrate the two subjects, first in your introduction (by putting them both in a single context) and again in your conclusion, where you should bring together the important points you have made about each. When discussing the second subject, try to refer repeatedly to your findings about the first ("In contrast to the rosy view of free trade offered by its supporters in the manufacturing sector, critics maintain that . . ."). This method may be the wisest choice if the subjects you are comparing seem so different that it is hard to create similar categories by which to discuss them.

If you can find similar criteria or categories for discussing both subjects, however, the comparison will be more effective if you organize it like this:

```
    resources:    negative views
                  positive views


manufacturing:    negative views
                  positive views


      culture:    negative views
                  positive views
```

Because this kind of comparison is more tightly integrated, it is easier for the reader to see the similarities and differences between the subjects. As a result, the essay is likely to be more forceful.

Arguing

The ability to present a case persuasively is an advantage in nearly every walk of life, not just in a formal debate, a law court, or a classroom. In an informal way, you likely argue regularly with fellow students or friends. However, an argument in a writing assignment is more challenging, especially when it deals with an emotionally charged or controversial issue.

All of us likely have some firm positions or points of view, especially in areas that have an explicit moral component or personally affect our lives. When we have strong feelings about something, probably others who disagree will have equally strong feelings. When arguments get heated, positions become even more entrenched and personal animosity comes to the fore. It was for this reason in days gone by that politics and religion were considered taboo subjects for the dinner table, since they undermined the calm civility of the gathering. Nowadays that taboo has disappeared, but we still have to recognize that arguments on controversial topics, where emotions or morals are involved, carry more risk. Consider how discussions about abortion or racism, to name just two examples, can become overheated and even violent. As Jonathan Haidt's recent research suggests, when facing an issue with moral implications, a person's immediate response is instinctive rather than rational; reasoning comes second.[4] What should you as a student do, then, when dealing with a controversial topic, sometimes not of your own choosing?

You may not be able to change the reader's mind, but you can win respect from your reader with the clarity and strength of your argument. You may be tempted from time to time simply to parrot the views of your professor, to argue what you think he or she wants to hear. This may work occasionally but it will not impress a discerning professor. How bored would you be after reading a number of papers repeating the same set of ideas you had already expressed? A better approach is to try to be as reasonable as possible in presenting your personal position.

Keep these guidelines in mind:

- Consider the opposing argument and likely points of disagreement. Rather than simply storming ahead with your own position, as if it is proof in itself, recognize the point of view or evidence that others may use against your case—then counter it. You can do this in several ways, such as creating an explicit list of misconceptions or "myths" versus your "reality." You may also begin your essay by acknowledging and explaining an alternative position and then continue with a detailed discussion of your own position and the evidence that supports it.
- Be as objective as possible in your wording. Avoid using loaded language up front that seems to prejudge your case or suggest a strong

bias. For example, avoid terms such as "his sentimental position" or "this hypocritical stance" when you have not yet given the evidence.

- Beware of a common fallacy in logical argument: the *ad hominem* attack—attacking the person rather than his or her ideas. One often encounters this fallacy in political or sociological discussions, such as dismissing a position on social welfare because the proponent is wealthy or on environmental legislation because the proponent is not a scientist. This is a lazy or "cheap" approach that undermines a reasoned case.

These suggestions do not mean that you should argue meekly or without conviction. Rather, a strong argument is one that is tightly reasoned and relies more on evidence than on feelings.

Writing introductions

The beginning of an essay has a dual purpose: to indicate your topic and the way you intend to approach it, and to whet your reader's interest in what you have to say.

The funnel approach

One effective way of introducing a topic is to place it in a context—to supply a kind of backdrop that will put it in perspective. The idea is to step back and discuss the area into which your topic fits and then gradually lead into your specific field of discussion. Sheridan Baker calls this the funnel approach, where a broad statement at the beginning narrows to the argument that you explain and develop in the body of your essay.[5]

For example, suppose that your topic is the growing moral maturity of Brian O'Connal in W.O. Mitchell's *Who Has Seen the Wind*. You might begin with a more general discussion of growing up in the West or of the movement from innocence to experience in other novels.

A funnel opening is applicable to almost any kind of essay. The following example is taken from an essay on the rise of complex society in Egypt:

> The great society of the Nile Valley that existed between about 3200 BCE and 600 BCE has aroused much public and professional interest. The spectacular pyramids and temples, however, have obscured the importance of the small predynastic villages in which Egyptian culture has its roots. The change from isolated family

communities to a more complex existence with a central authority took place rapidly. In 5000 BCE the Egyptians were hunters and part-time farmers, but a mere 1,600 years later they had diversified immensely. Although many general theories exist for the rise of the Nile Valley culture, this essay will show that no single factor is responsible. Rather, many different causes, from writing, warfare, religion, and agriculture to trade, social stratification, and foreign influences, all played a part.[6]

You should try to catch your reader's interest right from the start. You know from your own reading how a dull beginning can put you off a book or an article. The fact that your instructor must read on anyway makes no difference. If a reader has to get through thirty or forty similar essays, it's all the more important for yours to stand out.

A funnel opening isn't the only way to catch the reader's attention. The following are three of the most common leads.

The quotation

This approach works especially well when the quotation is taken from the person or work that you will be discussing. Here is an example from an essay on Virginia Woolf's *To the Lighthouse*:

> In *A Room of One's Own* Virginia Woolf sketches a "plan of the soul" for every individual, in which both male and female powers exist. "The normal and comfortable state of being," she suggests, is that "the two live in harmony together, spiritually co-operating." The main characters in *To the Lighthouse*, written two years earlier, struggle to attain this gender balance. Woolf shows that this inner harmony is constantly destroyed by the sexual attitudes of the day. She creates characters who were born androgynous, but whose natural balance is undermined by the strictures of society.

You can also use a quotation from an unrelated source or author, as long as it is relevant to your topic and not so well known that it will appear trite.

The question

A rhetorical question will annoy the reader if it's commonplace or if the answer is obvious, but a thought-provoking question can make a strong opening. For example, you might begin an essay on the issue of Aboriginal people's right to self-government with the question, "Does Aboriginal self-government mean better government?" Just be sure that you do actually answer the question somewhere in your essay.

The anecdote or telling fact

This is the kind of concrete lead that journalists often use to grab their readers' attention. For example, a sociology paper on young offenders might begin: "The bailiff leads Jimmy through a maze of corridors from the detention cell to the courtroom. A stranger to the halls of Keane County youth court would need a map, but Jimmy could probably find his way blindfolded; after all, he's made this trek more than a dozen times since he was ten." Save this approach for your least formal essays—and remember that the incident must really highlight the ideas you are going to discuss.

Whatever lead you use, it must relate to your topic: never sacrifice relevance for originality. Finally, whether your introduction is one paragraph or several, make sure that by the end of it your reader clearly knows the purpose of your essay and how you intend to accomplish it.

Writing conclusions

Endings can be painful—sometimes for the reader as much as for the writer. Too often, the feeling that one ought to say something profound and memorable produces a pretentious or affected ending. You know the sort of thing:

> Clearly the symbolism of *Four Quartets* is both intellectually and emotionally stimulating. Through it Eliot has produced poetry of lasting significance which will inspire readers for generations to come.

It's easy to see that these two sentences might better have been omitted.

Experienced editors say that many articles and essays would be better without their final paragraphs; in other words, when you have finished saying what you have to say, the best thing to do is to stop. This advice may work for short essays, where you need to keep the central point firmly in the foreground and don't need to remind the reader of it. However, for longer pieces, where you have developed a number of ideas or a complex line of argument, you should provide a sense of closure. Readers welcome an ending that helps to tie the ideas together; they don't like to feel as though they've been left dangling. And since the final impression is often the most lasting, it's in your interest to finish strongly. Simply restating your thesis or summarizing what you have already said isn't forceful enough. The following are some of the alternatives:

The inverse funnel

The simplest conclusion is one that restates the thesis *in different words* and then discusses its implications. Sheridan Baker calls this the *inverse funnel approach*, as opposed to the funnel approach of the opening paragraph.[7] In this type of conclusion, the specific arguments made in the body of the essay widen to a more inclusive final statement.

The essay on the rise of complex society in Egypt, which was cited earlier in the chapter for its funnel opening, concludes with an "inverse funnel":

> The evidence presented in this analysis suggests that writing, warfare, religion, agriculture, trade, and changes in the makeup of society all contributed to the rise of complex society in Egypt. It is hard to say which cause was the most important, and it is impossible to determine for certain the sequence of events. The most plausible theory, however, is that one factor in turn produced others. The effect is rather like that of a delicate ecosystem: one change in the environment will produce other reactions, and the greater the initial change, the greater the following ones will be. Egypt went through enormous changes during the third millennium BCE and, as with the changes of the last century, the effect was explosive and rapid in restructuring the culture.

One danger in moving to a wider perspective is that you may try to embrace too much. When a conclusion expands too far it tends to lose focus. It's always better to discuss specific implications than to trail off into vague generalities in an attempt to sound profound.

The new angle

A variation of the basic inverse funnel approach is to reintroduce your argument with a new twist. Suggesting some fresh angle can make your ending more compelling or provocative. Beware of introducing an entirely new idea, though, or one that's only loosely connected to your original argument; the result, if it's too far off-topic, could detract from your argument instead of enhancing it. The following is a short and very effective conclusion to an essay on Lawren Harris's spiritual landscapes, which shifts our attention to the artist's own words about them:

> The main inspiration for Harris's painting was a profoundly philosophical attitude to the Canadian North, expressed within the framework of theosophical thought. It was an attitude coloured by the ideas of Wassily Kandinsky and by his own basic romanticism. Harris once said, "No man is profound enough to explain fully the nature of his own inspiration" (Harris and Colgrove 7), a statement that undoubtedly reflects his understanding of the myriad of unconscious as well as conscious influences on an artist. Yet despite this reservation, Harris was more helpful than most artists in explaining what inspired and influenced those spiritual landscapes, which are central to his work and his reputation.

The full circle

If you began your essay by relating an anecdote, posing a rhetorical question, or citing a startling fact, you can complete the circle by referring to it again in your conclusion, relating it to some of the insights revealed in the main body of your essay. This technique provides a nice sense of closure for the reader.

The stylistic flourish

Some of the most successful conclusions end on a strong stylistic note. Try varying the sentence structure: if most of your sentences are long and complex, make the last one short and punchy, or vice versa. Sometimes you can dramatize your idea with a striking phrase or colourful image. When you are writing your essay, keep your eyes open and your ears tuned for fresh ways of putting things, and save the best for the end.

Integrating quotations

A quotation can benefit an essay in two ways. First, it adds depth and credibility by showing that your position or idea has the support of an authority. Second, it provides stylistic variety and interest, especially if the quotation is colourful or eloquent. The trick to using quotations effectively is to make sure that they are properly integrated with your own discussion—that they neither dominate your ideas nor seem tacked on. To ensure that a quotation has the desired effect, always refer to the point you want the reader to take from it; don't let a quotation dangle on its own. Usually, the best way to do this is to make the point before the quotation:

> During World War II, Mackenzie King tried to muddle through the conflict of those wanting conscription and those opposed to it by saying, "Conscription if necessary, but not necessarily conscription."

Sometimes, however, a quotation can precede the explanation. This is a common approach to beginning an essay, as illustrated earlier in this chapter. You must make sure, however, that you explain the significance of the quotation so that your reader is not left wondering why you have added it.

If a complete sentence precedes the quotation, use a colon at the end of the introductory phrase; otherwise use a comma:

> Margaret Thatcher stated her position firmly: "The lady's not for turning."

(or)

> Margaret Thatcher held to her position, insisting, "The lady's not for turning."

If the end of the quoted passage comes at the end of a sentence, finish with a period—unless the sentence is a question, in which case finish with a question mark after the quotation marks:

> Did her party believe her when she insisted that "The lady's not for turning"?

The length of a quotation can vary from a short phrase woven into the middle of a sentence to a paragraph or more. Just remember that the longer the quotation, the greater the danger that it will overshadow rather than reinforce your own viewpoint. Don't quote any more than you really need.

Avoiding plagiarism

Plagiarism is a form of stealing; as with other illegal offences, ignorance is no excuse. Penalties for plagiarism range from a grade of zero to outright expulsion. The way to avoid plagiarism is to give credit where credit is due. If you are using someone else's idea, acknowledge it, even if you have changed the wording or just summarized the main points. Don't be afraid that your work will seem weaker if you acknowledge the ideas of others. On the contrary, it will be all the more convincing; serious academic treatises are almost always built on the work of preceding scholars, with credit duly given to the earlier work.

Let's say you are assigned an essay on the expulsion of the French Acadians from Nova Scotia in 1755. The following is a passage from John Mack Faragher's book *A Great and Noble Scheme*:

> The removal of the Acadians. . . . was executed methodically by officers of the government in accordance with a carefully conceived plan many years in the making. It utilized all the available resources of the state. It included the seizure and destruction of Acadian records and registers, the arrest and isolation of community leaders, the separation of men from women and children. In the nineteenth century, operations of that kind would be directed at Indian peoples such as the Cherokees, but before 1755, nothing like it had been seen in North America. Today, the universal condemnation of ethnic cleansing by world opinion makes it difficult to defend what was done. In 2003, Queen Elizabeth II issued a Royal Proclamation acknowledging British responsibility for the decision to deport the Acadian people and regretting its "tragic consequences."[8]

One student's essay includes the following passage. It is plagiarized because exact phrasing is taken from the original and no acknowledgement is given:

✗ The expulsion of the Acadians in 1755 **included the seizure and destruction of Acadian records and registers, the arrest and isolation of community leaders, the separation of men from women and children.** It was in fact the first instance of **ethnic cleansing** in North America. **In 2003, Queen Elizabeth II issued a Royal Proclamation acknowledging British responsibility for the decision to deport the Acadian people and regretting its "tragic consequences."**

To avoid a charge of plagiarism and its unpleasant and sometimes disastrous consequences, all you need to do is acknowledge your source. In the correctly documented passage below, words and phrases taken directly from the original are in quotation marks, and a parenthetical text citation is included at the end of the passage. (See Chapter 7 for alternative citation styles.) A bibliography at the end of the essay gives complete publication information for the source.

✓ The expulsion of the Acadians in 1755 "included the seizure and destruction of Acadian records and registers, the arrest and isolation of community leaders, the separation of men from women and children." It was in fact the first instance of "ethnic cleansing" in North America. "In 2003, Queen Elizabeth II issued a Royal Proclamation acknowledging British responsibility for the decision to deport the Acadian people and regretting its 'tragic consequences.'" (Faragher xix).

The following passage is also plagiarized. This student has made the common mistake of assuming that putting the information in his own words is good enough. It's not. The concept of ethnic cleansing is still "borrowed":

✗ In 1755 the first instance of ethnic cleansing in North America occurred when officers of the government removed the Acadians from Nova Scotia using all the state resources at their disposal.

Remember that plagiarism involves not only using someone else's words but also expressing ideas that you got elsewhere without making it clear that they were taken from another source.

In the correctly documented passage below, proper acknowledgement takes the form of a reference to the author in text with the page number cited at the end of the relevant material:

✓ As historian John Mack Faragher argues in his book *A Great and Noble Scheme*, the first instance of ethnic cleansing in North America occurred in 1755 when officers of the government removed the Acadians from Nova Scotia using all the state resources at their disposal (xix).

Where should you draw the line on acknowledgements? As a rule, you don't need to give credit for anything that's common knowledge. You wouldn't footnote lines from "O Canada," for example, or the date of Confederation, but you should acknowledge any clever turn of phrase that is neither well known nor your own. And always document any fact or claim—statistical or otherwise—that is unfamiliar or open to question.

For students in a hurry, online material is a particular hazard and can cause a lot of grief. Even though websites are instantly accessible, the material is not common property. In fact, it is the property of the individual or organization that publishes it and is protected by copyright in the same way that printed material is. (Information about the proper procedure for documenting online material is included in Chapter 7.) It is crucial that you properly acknowledge the information you find on a website.

A warning: many instructors now use software programs that can detect plagiarism from both online and other sources. As these programs continue to improve, the likelihood of being caught increases. Although everyone likely knows of someone who lifts passages from the Internet or buys essays from an online seller, consider the ethics as well as the penalties and resist the temptation.

The Editing Stage

Often the best writer in a class is not the one who can dash off a fluent first draft but the one who is the best editor. To edit your work well you need to see it as the reader will, and in order to do that you have to distinguish between what you meant to say and what you have actually put on the page. For this reason it's a good idea to leave some time between drafts so that when you begin to edit you will be looking at the writing afresh rather than reviewing it from memory. This is the time to go to a movie or the gym or to do something that will take your mind off your work. Without this distancing period you can become so involved in your paper that it's hard to see your writing objectively.

Editing doesn't mean simply checking your work for errors in grammar or spelling. It means looking at the piece as a whole to see if the ideas are well organized, well documented, and well expressed. It may mean making changes to the structure of your essay by adding some paragraphs or sentences, deleting others, and moving others around. Experienced writers may be able to check several aspects of their work at the same time, but if you are inexperienced or in doubt about your writing, it's best to look at the organization of the ideas before you tackle sentence structure, diction, style, and documentation.

What follows is a checklist of questions to ask yourself as you begin editing. Far from all-inclusive, it focuses on the first step: examining the organization of your work. Since you probably won't want to check through your work separately for each question, you can group some together and overlook others, depending on your own strengths and weaknesses as a writer.

Checking for organization

- Is my title concise and informative?
- Are the purpose and approach of this essay evident from the beginning?
- Are all sections of the paper relevant to the topic?
- Is the organization logical?
- Are the ideas sufficiently developed? Is there enough evidence, explanation, and illustration?
- Would an educated person who hasn't read the primary material understand everything I'm saying? Should I clarify some parts or add any explanatory material?
- In presenting my argument, do I take into account opposing arguments or evidence?
- Do my paragraph divisions make my ideas more coherent? Have I used them to keep similar ideas together and signal movement from one idea to another?
- Do any parts of the essay seem disjointed? Should I add more transitional words or logical indicators to make the sequence of ideas easier to follow?
- Do my conclusions accurately reflect my argument in the body of the work?

Another approach would be to devise your own checklist based on comments you have received on previous assignments. This is particularly useful when you move from the overview of your paper to the close focus on sentence structure, diction, punctuation, spelling, and style. If you have a particular weak area—for example, irrelevant evidence or run-on sentences—you should give it special attention. Keeping a personal checklist will save you from repeating the same old mistakes.

Your word-processing program will catch typos as well as spelling errors, but remember that it may not point out actual words that are wrongly used (such as *there* when you need *their*). Think of the spell checker as a useful first check rather than a final one. Similarly, grammar checkers are not always reliable. They will pick up common grammar errors and stylistic problems, but they do make mistakes and will likely never equal the judgment of a good human editor.

Keep in mind, too, that for final editing most good writers suggest working from the printed page rather than from the computer screen. Print a draft and use the hard copy for your editing and proofreading. You will read more slowly and with greater acuity, and the final product will be more polished as a result.

Formatting Your Essay

We've all been told not to judge a book by its cover, but the very warning suggests that we have a natural tendency to do so. Readers of essays find the same thing. A well-typed, attractive essay creates a receptive reader and, fairly or unfairly, often gets a higher mark than a sloppy paper that is more difficult to read. Good looks won't substitute for good thinking, but they will certainly enhance it.

Most instructors will provide you with guidelines specifying their particular preferences for presentation and formatting. Unless you are directed otherwise, double space your work and use margins of at least one inch to frame the text in white space and allow room for your reader to write comments. Number each page and provide identifying information at the top of page one as follows:

```
Name
Course
Instructor's Name
Date
                              Title
```

Make good use of formatting features such as bold and italics for emphasis, and choose an appropriate, readable font.

Keep in mind that while a computer can make your work look good, fancy graphics and a slick presentation won't replace intelligent thinking. Read over your work with a critical eye and take the time to change anything that is unsatisfactory.

Protecting Your Work

Lost files are the nightmare of the computer age. Keeping adequate copies of your work will protect you from losing it as a result of a technical problem. The following practices will ensure that your work is adequately protected:

- Save regularly to protect against a computer failure.
- Create a backup so that you have copies on both your hard drive and a USB flash drive or a server.
- Keep a copy of your file at least until you receive your grade for the course.
- Print an extra copy just to be on the safe side.

Getting into the habit of following these steps is a good investment of your time and will give you valuable peace of mind.

Notes

1. For a more detailed discussion of heuristic procedures, see Richard E. Young, Alton L. Becker, and Kenneth Pike, *Rhetoric, Discovery and Change* (New York: Harcourt Brace Jovanovich, 1970), 119–36.
2. Joseph F. Trimmer, *Writing with a Purpose*, 12th ed. (Boston: Houghton Mifflin, 1998), 62–3.
3. John R. Trimble, *Writing with Style: Conversations on the Art of Writing* (Upper Saddle River, NJ: Prentice-Hall, 2000), 22–3.
4. Jonathan Haidt, *The Righteous Mind: Why Good People Are Divided by Politics and Religion* (New York: Random House, 2012).
5. Sheridan Baker and Laurence B. Gamache, *The Canadian Practical Stylist*, 4th ed. (Don Mills, ON: Addison-Wesley, 1998), 55–6.
6. We are grateful to Dr. Margaret Proctor for providing this and other samples of essay writing and to Elizabeth Holliday, Kate Saunders, and other former University of Toronto students, whose essays have been adapted for this purpose.
7. Baker and Gamache 63–5.
8. John Mack Faragher, *A Great and Noble Scheme: The Tragic Story of the Expulsion of the French Acadians from Their American Homeland* (New York: W.W. Norton & Company, 2005), xix. Excerpt copyright © 2005 by John Mack Faragher. Used by permission of W.W. Norton & Company, Inc.

3

Writing a Book Report

In this chapter, we will examine

- strategies for writing an informative book report;
- the components of an analytic book report; and
- guidelines for writing a literary review.

Introduction

The term *book report* covers a variety of writing assignments, from a simple summary of a book's contents to a sophisticated literary review. In between is the kind that you will most often be asked to produce: an analytic report containing some evaluation. The following guidelines cover the three basic kinds of book reports. Before you begin your assignment, be sure to check with your instructor to find out exactly which type is expected.

The Informative Book Report or Summary

The purpose of an *informative book report* is to summarize a book briefly and coherently. It is not intended to be evaluative; that is, it does not say anything about your reaction to the work. It simply records, as accurately as possible in as few words as possible, your understanding of what the author has written. It's not a complicated task, but it does call on your ability to get to the heart of things—to separate what is important from what is not. Aside from some pertinent publication information, all a simple informative report needs to be is an accurate summary of the book's contents.

Reading the book

Determine the author's purpose
An author writes a book for a reason. Usually it's to cast some new light on a subject, to propose a new theory, or to bring together the existing knowledge

in a field. Whatever the purpose, you have to discover it if you want to understand what guided the author's selection and arrangement of material. The best way to find out what the author intends to do is to check the table of contents, preface, and introduction.

Skim-read the book first

As noted on page 9, a quick overview of a book's contents will show you what the author considers most important and what kind of evidence he or she presents. The details will be much more understandable once you know where the book as a whole is going.

Reread carefully and take notes

A second, more thorough reading will be the basis of your note-taking. Since you have already determined the relative importance that the author gives to various ideas, you can be selective and avoid getting bogged down in less important details. Just be sure that you don't neglect any crucial passages or controversial claims.

When taking notes, try to condense the ideas. Don't take them down word for word, and don't simply paraphrase them. You will have a much firmer grasp of the material if you resist the temptation to quote; force yourself to interpret and summarize. This approach will also help you make your report concise. Remember: you want to be brief as well as clear. Condensing the material as you take notes will ensure that your report is a true summary, not just a string of quotations or paraphrases.

Writing the report

Identify primary and secondary ideas

When writing your report, give the same relative emphasis to each area as the author does. Don't just list the topics in the book or the conclusions reached; discriminate between primary ideas and secondary ones.

Follow the book's order of presentation

A simple summary doesn't have to address topics in the same order in which they are presented in the book, but it's usually safer to follow the author's lead. That way your summary will be a clear reflection of the original.

Follow the logical chain of the arguments
Don't leave any confusing holes in your summary. You won't be able to cover every detail, of course, but you must make sure to trace all the main arguments in such a way that they make sense.

Include the key evidence supporting the author's arguments
Remember to include the evidence the author uses to support his or her arguments. Without some supporting details, your reader will have no way of assessing the strength of the author's conclusions.

Tailor the length to fit your needs
A summary can be any length, from one page to six or seven pages. It depends less on the length of the original material than on your purpose. If the report is an assignment, find out how long your instructor wants it to be. If it's for personal reference only, you will have to decide how much detail you want to have on hand.

Read and revise your report to make sure it's coherent
Summaries can often seem choppy or disconnected because so much of the original material is left out. Use linking words and phrases (see pages 143–4) to help create a flow and give your writing a sense of logical development. Careful paragraph division will also help to frame the various sections of the summary. If the report is for a science, social science, or business course, you can probably use headings to identify sections.

Edit your report carefully
You may find that you have to edit your work a number of times to eliminate unnecessary words and get your report down to the required length. Editing can be a difficult task, but it becomes easier with practice.

Include publication details
Details about the book (publisher, place and date of publication, and number of pages) must appear somewhere in your report, whether at the beginning or at the end. Follow the guidelines in Chapter 7 for presenting these details in the correct manner.

The Analytic Book Report

An *analytic book report*—sometimes called a book review—not only summarizes the main ideas in a book but at the same time evaluates them. It's best to begin with an introduction and then follow with a summary and an evaluation. Publication details are usually listed at the beginning but can also be placed at the end.

Introduction

In your introduction you should provide all the background information necessary for a reader who is not familiar with the book. Here are some of the questions you might consider:

- What is the book about? Is the title pertinent and useful as a guide to the book's contents?
- What is the author's purpose? What kind of audience is he or she writing for? How is the topic limited? Is the central theme or argument stated or only implied?
- How does this book relate to others in the same field?
- What is the author's background? Reputation? What other books or articles has he or she written?
- Are there any special circumstances connected with the writing of this book? For example, was it written with the cooperation of particular scholars or institutions? Does the subject have special significance for the author?
- What kind of evidence does the author present to support his or her ideas? Is it reliable and current?

Not all of these questions will apply to every book, but an introduction that answers some of them will put your reader in a much better position to appreciate what you have to say in your evaluation.

Summary

You cannot analyze a book without discussing its contents. The basic steps are the same as those outlined above for the informative book report. You may present a condensed version of the book's contents as a separate section, followed by your evaluation, or you may integrate the two, assessing the author's arguments as you present them.

Evaluation

In evaluating the book, you will want to consider some of the following questions:

- How is the book organized? Does the author focus too much on some areas and too little on others? Has anything been left out?
- How has the author divided the work into chapters? Are the divisions valid? Do the chapter titles accurately reflect each chapter's contents?
- What kind of assumptions does the author make in presenting the material? Are they stated or implied? Are they valid?
- Does the author accomplish what he or she sets out to do? Does the author's position change during the course of the book? Are there any contradictions or weak spots in the arguments? Does the author recognize those weaknesses or omissions?
- What documentation does the author provide to support the central theme or argument? Is it reliable and current? Is any of the evidence distorted or misinterpreted? Could the same evidence be used to support a different case? Does the author leave out any important evidence that might weaken his or her case? Is the author's position convincing?
- Does the author agree or disagree with other writers who have dealt with the same material or problem? In what respect?
- Is the book clearly written and interesting to read? Is the writing repetitious? Too detailed? Not detailed enough? Is the style clear? Or is it plodding, flippant, or weighed down with jargon?
- Does the book raise issues that need further exploration? Does it present any challenges or leave unfinished business for the author or other scholars to pursue?
- If the book has an index, how good is it?
- Are there illustrations? Are they helpful?
- To what extent would you recommend this book? How has it affected your views on the topic?

Remember that your job is not to interpret the content of the book but to indicate its strengths and weaknesses. Also, be sure that you review the book the author actually wrote, not the one you wish he or she had written. In short, be fair.

The Literary Review

The *literary review* is a variation of the analytic book report. Although litera-ture is its most frequent subject, it may deal with a wide range of topics, from art and music to the social sciences. The term *literary* refers to the style of the review rather than to the material discussed; the review should stand on its own merit as an attractive piece of writing. Reviews for most courses relate to books. However, in some subjects, such as fine arts, instructors may want a more specific format for a review of works rather than books. It's a good idea to check before starting.

The advantage of a literary review is the freedom it allows you in both content and presentation. You may emphasize any aspect you like, as long as you leave your reader with a basic understanding of what the book is about. Remember that your job is not to give a plot summary. In most cases, your purpose is simply to provide a graceful introduction to the work based on your personal assessment of its most intriguing—or annoying—features. Be careful, though, not to make it too personal; some reviewers end up telling us more about themselves than about the book. Although a literary review is usually less comprehensive than an analytic report, it should always be thoughtful, and your judgment must never be superficial.

The best way of learning how to write good literary reviews is to read some of them. Check the book review sections of a magazine such as *Maclean's* or the weekend edition of the *Globe and Mail* to see different approaches. Pay particular attention to the various techniques that reviewers use to catch the reader's interest and hold it. The basic rule is to reinforce your comments with specific details from the book; concrete examples will add authenticity and life to your review.

4

Writing a Lab Report

> **In this chapter, we will examine**
> - the importance of writing for a specific purpose and reader;
> - the standard sections and order of a lab report; and
> - the characteristics of an effective writing style for scientific reports.

Introduction

Students in the sciences and social sciences are often asked to report formally on the results of scientific experiments. Although lab reports generally conform to a basic format, each discipline (chemistry, physics, biology, psychology, etc.) has slightly different requirements.

Any kind of academic writing should be clear, concise, and forceful. For scientific writing there is one more imperative: be objective. Scientists are interested in exact information and the orderly presentation of factual evidence to support theories or hypotheses. Although you may wish to make a case for a particular hypothesis, it is essential to separate the facts you are reporting from your own speculations about them. You must never allow your preconceived opinions or expectations to interfere with the way you collect or present your data. If you do, you run the risk of distorting your results. You must conduct your experiment as objectively as possible and present the results in such a way that anyone who reads your report or attempts to duplicate your procedure will be likely to reach the same conclusions that you did.

Purpose and Reader

As an undergraduate, you will most often write lab reports to demonstrate that you understand a theory or phenomenon or that you know how to test a certain hypothesis. Since your reader is your instructor, you can assume that he or she will be familiar with scientific terms; therefore, you do not need to define or explain them. You can also assume that your reader will be on the lookout for any weaknesses in methodology or analysis and any omissions of important data. Usually you will be expected to give details of your calculations, but even when all you have been asked to provide are the results of your calculations, you should be sure to note any irregularities in the experiment that might affect the accuracy of your results.

Format

Since the information in scientific reports must be easy for the reader to find, it should be organized into separate sections, each with a heading. One of the differences between writing lab reports and writing essays is that in a report you should use headings and subheadings whenever possible, as well as graphs, tables, or diagrams (see Chapter 6). By convention, most lab reports follow a standard order:

1. title page
2. *Abstract* (or *Summary*)
3. *Introduction* (or *Purpose* or *Objective*)
4. *Materials* (or *Equipment Setup*)
5. *Method*
6. *Results*
7. *Discussion* (or *Analysis*)
8. *Conclusions*
9. attachments or appendices
10. *References*

The order of these sections is always the same, although some sections may be combined or given slightly different names, depending on how much information you have in each one. Different disciplines also have slightly different rules, but the following will give you an overview of what should go into each section of your report.

Title page
The first page of the report is your title page. It should include your name, the title of the experiment, the date on which it was performed, and the date of submission; for practical purposes it should also include the name of your

course and instructor. Your title should be brief—no more than 10 or 12 words—but informative, and it should clearly describe the topic and scope of your experiment. Avoid meaningless phrases, such as "A study of . . ." or "Observations on . . ."; simply state what it is you are studying, such as "The effects of background music on the attention span of hyperactive children." Sometimes you may want to emphasize the result you obtained, for example, "Background music played at a low volume increases the attention span of hyperactive children."

Abstract

The *Abstract* appears on a separate page following the title page. It is a brief but comprehensive summary of your report that should be able to stand alone; that is, someone should be able to read it and know exactly what the experiment was about as well as what the results were and how you interpreted them. Your summary should describe the purpose of the experiment, the experimental materials, the procedure, the results, and your conclusions. For a simple experiment your *Abstract* may be only a few lines, but even for a complex one you should keep it to about 200 words. For this reason, you should avoid vague or wordy phrases, such as "The reason for conducting the experiments in this study of X was to examine . . ." when you can be more concise: "X was studied to examine the effect of . . ."

Introduction

The *Introduction* gives a more detailed statement of purpose or objective. It should describe the problem you are studying, the reasons for studying it, and the research strategy you used to obtain the relevant data. If, as is often the case, your purpose is to test a hypothesis about a specific problem, you should state clearly both the nature of the problem and what you expected to find. Your *Introduction* should include the theory underlying the experiment and any pertinent background data or equations. Although you may refer to papers relevant to the experiment, it's best to avoid quoting extensively.

Materials

The *Materials* section should contain a description of the materials and equipment you used and some explanation of how the experiment was set up. If you used different arrangements of the equipment for different parts of the experiment, give a full list of the equipment in this section, and in the *Method* section describe each separate arrangement before you outline the procedure for which it was used. When the description of the materials is short, you may combine this section with the *Method* section. Many departments encourage students in first- and second-year courses to have a single *Materials and Method* section.

A simple diagram—produced on computer or by hand—will help the reader visualize the arrangement of the equipment. If the diagram is too large to fit a regular page, you can prepare it as an appropriately labelled attachment at the back of the report and refer to it within the body of the report.

If the apparatus or materials you are using consist of standard, commercially available items, some departments require that you specify the name of the manufacturer, the model number (if applicable), and the name of the source or supplier. Such information should be included in this section, for example, "Spectroscopic-grade carbon tetrachloride (99 per cent pure) was obtained from BDH Chemicals."

Method

The *Method* section is a step-by-step description of how you carried out the experiment, with the procedures described in the order in which you actually performed them. If your experiment consisted of a number of tests, you should begin this section with a short summary statement listing the tests so that the reader will be prepared for the series. When you describe the tests later on in the report, discuss them in the same order to avoid confusion.

This part of your report must be written with enough detail so that others would have no difficulty repeating the experiment in all its essential details. If you are following instructions in a lab manual, you should not copy them out word for word, since this might be considered plagiarism. You may be permitted simply to refer to the instructions and give details of any deviation, but verify this with your lab instructor. When a certain procedure is long, complicated, or not necessary to a full understanding of the experiment, you may describe it in a labelled attachment at the end of the report.

Although you should be concise in your description of the experimental method, make sure that you don't omit essential details. If you heated a test tube, for example, you must report at what temperature it was heated and for how long. If you performed a chromatography or other process at a faster or slower rate than usual, you must indicate the rate. Readers must know exactly what controls to apply if they try to perform the experiment themselves.

When describing experiments, it is standard practice to use the past tense. There is no clear consensus, however, on whether to use active or passive voice (e.g., "*I heated* the beaker" versus "The beaker *was heated*"). Traditionally, only the passive voice was used for this kind of writing because it emphasizes the procedure rather than the person. More recently, there has been a tendency to use the active voice because it is clearer and less likely to produce awkward, convoluted sentences. Ask your instructor about the department's preferences, but also use your own judgment about what sounds best. Your goal, whichever voice you use, is to achieve clarity and objectivity.

Results

This is the section of most interest to scientists, and they depend on its accuracy. It usually contains a mix of data and verbal description. It will also likely contain some statistical calculations.

Find out from your instructor whether you are expected to give the details of your calculations or only the results of those calculations. In either case, you should pay special attention to the units of any quantities; to omit or misuse them is a serious scientific mistake. Taking care to include all units will also reveal mistakes in your calculations that might otherwise go undetected. If your units don't cancel properly to yield the result you expect, you will know that you have made an error.

You should also make sure where possible that the calculated values you report include the *uncertainty* in each of them. For example, you might report that the calculated volume of a hollow sphere is 23.45 ± 0.05 cc (where ± 0.05 is the uncertainty in the volume measurement). When reporting any calculations or measurements, check to see if you need to include the standard deviation, the standard error of the mean, or the coefficient of variation.

The format of the *Results* section depends on the type of experiment performed. Generally, it begins with the main finding and then deals with secondary ones. Whenever possible, summarize your results in a graph or table. A graph is usually preferable to a table since it has greater visual impact. However, if you have made several measurements, you might not be able to include your results in a single figure and are probably best to report them in tabular form. Whatever type of figure or table you use, label it clearly and be sure to refer to it and explain it in the text. Today's computer programs have sophisticated charting features. See Chapter 6 for a discussion of graphs and tables.

Remember the following guidelines when you are creating graphs for your lab report:

- Use a scale that will allow you to distribute your data points as widely as possible on the page.
- Put the independent variable (the one you have manipulated) on the horizontal axis and the dependent variable (the one you measure) on the vertical axis.
- Make the vertical axis about three-quarters the length of the horizontal axis.
- Use large and distinctive symbols, with different symbols for each line on the graph.
- Put error bars (±) on data points where possible.
- Label the axes clearly and always include the units of measurement used so that the reader knows exactly what you have plotted on the graph. You can also include a legend to indicate the different units or to explain what the different symbols represent.
- Give the graph a title and caption (for example, "Figure 1") so that you can refer to it by number in your report.

Discussion

The *Discussion* section of the lab report allows you the greatest freedom, since it is here that you analyze and interpret the test results and comment on their significance. You should show how the test produced its outcome—whether expected or unexpected—and discuss those elements that influenced the results. In determining what details to include in the analysis section, you might try to answer the following questions:

- Do the results reflect the objective of the experiment?
- Do the results agree with previous findings as reported in the literature on the subject? If not, how can you account for the discrepancy between your own data and the values accepted or obtained by other students and scientists?
- What (if anything) may have gone wrong during your experiment and why? What was the source of any error?
- Could the results have another explanation?
- Did the procedures you used help you accomplish the purpose of the experiment? Does your experience in this experiment suggest a better approach for next time?

For a good discussion, remember to think critically not only about your own work but about how it relates to previous work.

Conclusions

The *Conclusions* section is a brief statement of the conclusions that may be drawn from the experiment. You don't necessarily need a separate section for your conclusions; they can also appear as a short summary at the end of the *Discussion* section. You may include a chart (table or graph) if you think it will clarify your conclusions.

Attachments

In some cases you may wish to include various data such as detailed calculations, measurements, and weights as attachments or appendices. These should be placed on separate pages at the end of the report.

References

The only way to avoid suspicion of plagiarism is to support every non-original statement with a reference citation. Each time you refer to a book or an article in the text of your report, cite the reference; then at the end of the paper, make a list of all the sources you have cited. The precise format of the citations and reference list varies among disciplines, so you should check with your instructor or department to see which style is preferred. If you are using endnotes to cite references, you will need to have a separate *Endnotes* section preceding the *References*. For details on the correct form for scientific documentation, see Chapter 7.

Writing Style

Scientific reports, like essays, must be written with the reader in mind. Since your reader is your instructor, you don't need to define basic scientific terms or explain a method that would be familiar to anyone with scientific training. At the same time, you should avoid filling your report with technical jargon when non-technical language will do the job. The guiding principles are clarity and precision: your goal is to make it as easy as possible for the reader to understand exactly what you mean.

Although the basic rules for writing a lab report are the same as for any other kind of writing, scientific reports do pose special problems for students. Here are a few words of advice:

Avoid using too many nouns as adjectives

Clusters of nouns used as adjectives can create cumbersome phrases:

orig.   adult male kidney disease

rev.   kidney disease in adult males

orig.   apparatus construction

rev.   construction of the apparatus

Of course, some nouns are frequently and quite acceptably used as adjectives, for example, _kidney_ disease, _hydrogen_ bomb, _reaction_ time, _S.I._ units. Your ear is probably the best judge of what is clear and what is not.

Avoid using too many abstract nouns

Whenever possible, choose a verb rather than an abstract noun:

orig.   The <u>addition</u> of acid and subsequent <u>agitation</u> of the solution resulted in the <u>formation</u> of crystals.

rev.   When acid <u>was added</u> and the solution <u>shaken</u>, crystals formed (passive).

rev.   When I <u>added</u> acid to the solution and <u>shook</u> it, crystals formed (active).

Avoid vague qualifiers

As a scientist you must be exact. In particular, you should avoid words such as *quite, very, fairly, some,* or *many* when you can use a more precise term. The word *relatively* is especially dangerous unless you are actually comparing two or more things.

Avoid unnecessary passive constructions

As noted on page 49, there is some debate among scientists about whether it is more appropriate to use the active voice or the passive voice to describe an experiment. Even if you prefer to use passive verbs for describing methods and results, you should try to use active verbs in your *Introduction* and in your *Discussion* and *Conclusions* sections. Your sentences will be clearer and more direct:

orig. pH4 <u>is needed</u> for the enzyme.

rev. The enzyme <u>needs</u> pH4.

orig. It <u>was reported</u> by E.A. Robinson that . . .

rev. E.A. Robinson <u>reported</u> that . . .

Avoid ambiguous pronouns

A pronoun will cause confusion if the reader can't tell which noun it refers to:

orig. The seed required water to germinate. <u>It</u> must be warm.

Is it the seed or the water that must be warm? If there is any chance of ambiguity, you should repeat the noun:

rev. The <u>water</u> must be warm.

(or)

rev. The <u>seed</u> must be warm.

Be especially careful that the demonstrative pronoun *this* clearly refers to a specific noun:

orig. When water was withheld, the stalk lost its leaves. <u>This</u> occurred over eight hours.

rev. When water was withheld, the stalk lost its leaves. <u>This loss</u> occurred over eight hours.

5

Writing a Business Report

In this chapter, we will examine

- specific strategies for planning a report;
- the sections of a business report and the arrangement of points within each section; and
- tips for effective report writing, including how to use headings, lists, and illustrations.

Introduction

In many business courses you will have to write the kind of formal report used in the business world. Most of these course reports are hypothetical exercises designed primarily to see if you understand the process of writing an actual report. Details of the report will depend on the circumstances, but the guidelines offered in this chapter will give you the general strategies and techniques for writing effective business reports, whether in school or on the job.

First Principles

Business managers with many demands on their time want to know the central idea of a report as quickly as possible. They also want to trust in its accuracy. When writing a business report, therefore, try to follow three basic principles:

1. Put the most important information up front, unless you have a particular reason to do otherwise. In most cases it's a good idea to put the essence of what you want to say in your first page or two—just in case that's all a busy reader happens to read.
2. Be concise. A report should say as much as possible in as little space as possible.

3. Be objective. Readers must be confident that the information you are providing is free of personal bias. Logical analysis will make your work believable (see pages 64–5).

Planning the Report

Defining the task: the four Rs

A business report that is vague or off-target will be of little interest to the reader and will more likely be filed than acted on. To create a focused and effective report, you need to plan carefully. As in any other kind of writing, taking time to organize your thoughts and devise your strategies is well worth the effort. The first step is to define precisely what it is that you have to do. Even if you are writing a hypothetical report as a course exercise, you still have to define the task as if it were the real thing. Before you even begin to write, examine the task by asking questions about four points: *Reason, Reader, Restrictions,* and *Research*.

What is the reason?

Why are you writing this report? What goal is it supposed to achieve? Broadly speaking, every report has one of two basic purposes: to provide information or to recommend some course of action. Many informational reports, such as progress reports, production reports, and monthly sales reports, are used regularly to pass along facts as they accumulate. Typically, these reports are fairly routine. On the other hand, reports that are written to make specific recommendations—to help someone make a decision or to suggest a solution to a particular problem—usually receive close attention from both writer and reader. Examples are proposals for a new product line, a feasibility study on a proposed plant location, or suggestions for reversing a sales decline. Fortunately, this is the kind of analytical report you will be asked to write for most courses. It provides an opportunity for you as the writer to show your ability to make inferences and judgments—both marks of managerial competence.

Determining the reason for such a report means establishing both its purpose and its expected outcome. If an important decision rests on your report, you will have to consider exactly what information is needed to make that decision and precisely how you will support any recommendations.

Who is the reader?

Although a report may be read by several people, it is usually aimed at one primary reader. Identifying this reader will enable you to organize and present your material in such a way that it is likely to be well received. Your instructor will analyze your work from a business perspective, so direct the report to the person you would be targeting if the report were real, not to the person who will grade it. Among the details you should consider are these:

- **What type of person is the reader?** Often the reaction to your report will depend less on the reader's job than on his or her personality. A cautious, conservative person might favour a carefully understated position, whereas a bold, creative type might prefer a more daring approach. If your personal knowledge of the reader is slight, you should try to find a reliable source to give you a few hints.
- **What is your relationship to the reader?** Is the reader your boss or a colleague? How has he or she reacted to past communications with you? If someone is in a position much higher than yours, your tone and approach should be more formal than they would be for an associate you talk to often.
- **Has the reader asked for the report?** If you are writing in response to a request, you may not need to fill in much detail about the purpose; if, however, the report is unsolicited, you should take care to place it in context.
- **What is the reader's area of expertise or responsibility?** You need to go into more detail about an area that is your reader's specialty than you would for a subject in which he or she is less interested or involved. Usually top management will want an overview, whereas a specialist will require all the particulars.

    In the business world your report might be going to several different kinds of readers—to a plant supervisor, for instance, as well as to top management. If so, you could consider giving the complete analysis to the supervisor and sending top management only an executive summary.
- **How is the reader likely to respond to the report?** Consider the reader's situation and the expectations and concerns that he or she is likely to have. If you can anticipate probable objections or concerns and answer them in the report itself, your work will be much more convincing.

- **How might the reader benefit from the report?** Your suggestions will be more persuasive if you can point out their advantages for the reader. The benefit could be significant: giving the reader a competitive edge in the marketplace, for example, or saving the business from impending financial collapse. Even if the benefit is a more general one, such as improving the reader's ability to anticipate future problems, you should point it out.

What are the restrictions*?*

From the outset, you should consider the practical restrictions on your writing. For example, how much time do you have? How much help is available for producing illustrations and other graphics, creating models, and printing and binding?

Other restrictions will apply specifically to the subject of the report. Because it's always better to do a thorough job on a narrow subject than a superficial job on a broad one, you must limit your topic to manageable proportions. If you are doing a report on newspaper readership, for example, you could consider restricting the scope of your study to a particular time frame (a specific year or years), a particular place (a certain region), a particular demographic (a certain market), or a particular kind of newspaper (dailies or weeklies).

At the same time, you should take into account the reader's time restrictions. For instance, it would be an annoying waste of his or her time to include, in a marketing plan for a small business, an option for television advertising that is too expensive to consider seriously. Careful focusing of the topic will spare your reader the trouble of going through unnecessary material.

What research *is required?*

In deciding what information to gather, you should weigh the time and money required to do the research against its usefulness to the report. In other words, you must determine what is essential.

Research decisions will be easier if you work out your topic in precise terms. A topic such as *A Report on Computers* is too vague to be useful. Be more specific: *A Cost-Benefit Analysis of Three Accounting Software Programs for the Accounting Department of Dominion Appliances.* You should then consider research needs in relation to the first three Rs: *Reason, Reader,* and *Restrictions.*

It is especially useful to determine how much your reader already knows. In many cases he or she will need no background information at all. If you must provide some, remember that too much detail will draw attention away from more important matters. One solution to this problem is to attach a short background section as an appendix at the end of the report.

Once you have decided on the information you need, you should ask yourself what, if anything, you have to verify. Is your source reliable? Should you cross-check any facts or figures? Remember that a source with a special interest in the matter may either exaggerate or minimize certain issues. Statistics themselves may not lie, but they can be manipulated to distort the true picture.

Finally, you should determine the degree of accuracy or precision required for any figures you supply. Indicating the margin of error will show the reader that you are thorough and objective.

Often the facts and figures you need can be obtained internally, either by questioning people on the job or by researching company documents. If you find that an earlier report covers some of the same material you are working on, you can refer to it and make use of the facts and figures you need, updating as necessary. If more extensive research is required, you may wish to consult relevant government documents, company reports, or academic studies available at a library or on the Internet. Most companies today have websites that give you easy access to annual reports, corporate information, product announcements, and financial information. (Remember that when you use another person's material you must acknowledge it and give proper references; see Chapter 7 for instructions on documenting your sources correctly.)

If you have to obtain your own data—through a questionnaire or survey, for example—make sure that any statistical results are based on an appropriate sample. If you aren't familiar with proper sampling methods yourself, consult someone who is; nothing will weaken your credibility more than providing unreliable or invalid statistical information.

Collaborating on a group report

You may be asked to write a report produced by a group. Sometimes the group can be self-selected, and members are free to form a compatible team. More often, as a simulation of work in the business world, the instructor will form the groups. In either case, a group report can be a source of satisfaction or of tension. Since organizations increasingly rely on team projects, this type of assignment is a worthwhile experience.

Good planning is essential. From the start, appoint one person as the overall coordinator who is responsible for organizational matters and for seeing that deadlines are met. Often this is not the best writer or the person with the most knowledge but rather the best people manager. Assign members to various parts of the project, from specific research or fact-finding to drafting a particular section or sections of the report. One person should handle the overall editing to ensure consistency of content and style. The editor's word should rule over the final draft.

In delegating tasks, try to make the burden of work as fair as possible—even though fairness is an elusive goal. Most of the complaints about collaborative writing are that one person has done more work than others—or has done a lot less—even though everyone gets the same grade. Remember, though, that this is no different from most team sports, where athletes recognize the advantages of collaboration despite differences in talent and experience. Even if you think you could do a better job writing and editing on your own, you likely could not be as quick or effective as a hardworking group, and you certainly would learn less about the challenges and rewards of teamwork. Whatever the apparent inequities, therefore, assume part of the responsibility for making the collaborative writing project a success.

Organizing your information

The trend today is to place the most important information—your recommendations or conclusions—first in a *Summary* or *Executive Summary*. Major consulting firms and others who routinely use this approach have found that it appeals to most readers because it gives them the highlights of the report at the outset.

A more indirect approach leads to the recommendations gradually, showing the reader in a careful, step-by-step way how you reached your conclusions. This approach is sometimes used if the reader's response might be unfavourable. As with any piece of writing, let the context and the intended audience be your guide.

Regardless of which approach you take, the body of your report should typically contain the following parts:

- **Summary.** The *Summary*—also called the *Executive Summary*—is a synopsis of the report. It is placed at the front of the report, on a separate page with a heading. The *Summary* usually highlights the most important information in the report, typically the conclusions or recommendations, and should be designed as a stand-alone piece for the reader who wants only a general overview of the main points. For this reason, you will probably find it easier to write the *Summary* last, after you have completed the report.

In writing the *Summary*, follow the order of the report. For a direct approach, put your conclusions and recommendations first. If you're trying to gain acceptance or approval, use an indirect approach and put the purpose and methodology first, and then gradually lead up to the conclusions and recommendations.

- **Introduction.** This section may include a statement of purpose, a brief discussion of the background or the reason for the report, and/or an explanation of the method used to gather the information.
- **Conclusions and/or Recommendations.** Conclusions are the inferences you have drawn from your findings; recommendations are suggestions about what actions to take. Depending on your reasons for writing the report, you may have conclusions or recommendations or both in this section, and the title you give it will vary accordingly.

  If your report uses an indirect approach, move this section down so that it follows the *Discussion of Findings*.
- **Discussion of Findings.** This section discusses the details of your investigation. It forms the longest section of most reports.

Organizing the details

The principle of "important things first" also applies to the arrangement of points within each section. In the *Recommendations* section especially, it's a good idea to put your most important point first, followed by the remaining points in descending order of importance.

Still, you should always keep in mind your purpose and reader. For example, if you are trying to persuade a hostile or skeptical reader, it may be better to begin with the point—major or minor—that will get the most favourable reaction. In the *Discussion of Findings* section—usually the most detailed part of a report—you may be better off letting your purpose determine the way you arrange the details, especially if the section is long. The following examples illustrate some common approaches to organizing the information in the body of your report:

- to present a benefits plan, you could *divide* or *classify* the information according to the different types of employee or different benefits;

- to describe a process, you could present the stages in *chronological* order;
- to discuss different markets for a product, you could follow a *spatial* order, arranging your findings according to geographical regions.

Ordering for comparison

When you are presenting information on which a choice will be based, you should order it in such a way that the reader will be able to compare the options easily. For example, suppose that you have been asked to recommend a new network server for an office and are considering three models: *Server X, Server Y,* and *Server Z.* The comparisons will be clearer for your reader and an assessment easier to make if, instead of presenting the strengths and weaknesses of each model in turn, you first decide on the criteria for comparison, and then for each criterion compare all three models. With four criteria—processor speed, memory, technical support, and price—the plan for the *Discussion of Findings* section might look like this:

A. Server X has the fastest processor.
   1. Server X
   2. Server Y
   3. Server Z

B. Server X has the most memory.
   1. Server X
   2. Server Y
   3. Server Z

C. Server Y has the best technical support.
   1. Server X
   2. Server Y
   3. Server Z

D. Server Z is the least expensive.
   1. Server X
   2. Server Y
   3. Server Z

Whichever way you choose to order the details, remember to be systematic and consistent. In addition, it's a good idea to include a graph or table to illustrate the points of comparison (see Chapter 6).

Beginnings

An internal office report may require nothing more than a memo heading. For more formal reports, however, you will have to supply some or all of the following elements.

Title page

The title you choose should be as precise and descriptive as possible so that the reader knows exactly what the report is about. A title such as *Feasibility Study: Plant Location* doesn't tell the reader very much; something like *A Comparison of Possible Central Ontario Locations for the Monarch Auto Parts Plant* is much better. The title page should also indicate who requested the report, who wrote it, and the date of presentation:

> Prepared for Riva Kirsh, President
> Monarch Industries Ltd.
> by
> Alan Soo
> Ace Consultants
> 4 May 2014

If you're writing the report for a course assignment, don't forget to include the necessary academic information, such as course name or number.

Letter of transmittal

The letter of transmittal is a personal letter or memo to the intended reader. It is sometimes attached to the front of the report, but it may also be placed after the title page, before the *Executive Summary*.

The letter usually opens with a sentence about the context of the report and then moves to a brief outline of the report's main features. It may then acknowledge the help of others in preparing the report. Usually it closes with a goodwill statement looking to the future. Here is an illustration:

> Last summer you asked the Student Affairs Committee to investigate campus security. Here is the report on our investigation.
>
> Our main recommendation is that the Student Council, with the cooperation of the Student Volunteer Bureau, establish an evening escort service to safeguard students walking across isolated areas of the campus at night. This service would benefit not only part-time and extension

students going home from classes but also students who need to work late in the library or computer labs.

   We are grateful for the support of your administrative assistant, Felicia Penofsky, whose suggestions were extremely helpful to us in conducting our investigation.

   When you have had the time to read and think about our recommendations, we would welcome the chance to discuss them with you.

In some cases the letter of transmittal provides a complete summary of the report, replacing the *Executive Summary*.

Table of contents

A table of contents is helpful in a long report because it allows the reader to find specific information quickly. Formats may vary. To make it as clear as possible, you should number each section of your report and include these numbers together with the appropriate section titles in the table of contents. Indent any subheadings, and place the page numbers for all sections and subsections in a corresponding column on the right.

Endings

After the main body of your report, you may include one or both of the following sections.

References

The *References* section should include detailed information about any documents, published or unpublished, used in preparing the report. Items should be listed by author in alphabetical order. You have several options for formatting this section, as outlined in Chapter 7; however, it's usually wisest to follow the conventions of your organization or the guidelines provided by your instructor.

Appendix

An appendix contains any material which substantiates claims made in the report but which is not essential to the report. An appendix might include additional tables, the questionnaire used in a survey, summaries of raw data, parts of other reports that are pertinent to your findings, or any other information that would slow the reader down unnecessarily if it appeared in the main text.

Writing the Report

As with any other kind of writing, business writing should be clear, concise, and forceful (see Chapter 11). Here are some additional guidelines that are especially useful for business reports:

Be objective

A business report must be as free as possible of bias and subjective opinions. Your reader will be more likely to accept your findings if you follow these suggestions:

- **Identify your assumptions.** If you are comparing computers, for example, and you assume that audio is not a factor, you should say so.
- **Avoid unsubstantiated judgments.** Be sure that any suggestions you make or conclusions you reach follow from the information you have given. Never imply anything that you cannot prove. If your findings aren't foolproof, show where the uncertainty lies.
- **Avoid subjective language.** Words such as *terrible* or *fantastic* detract from the objective tone you want. Instead of saying "sales have shown an amazing increase," give the exact percentage of the increase and let the facts speak for themselves.

The overall tone to aim for depends on the circumstances—particularly the intended reader. If you are writing a short, informal report to someone you see often, familiar terms such as *I* or *you* are appropriate. On the other hand, many formal reports try to avoid the subjective impression created by personal pronouns. The result, unfortunately, is often a cumbersome load of passive constructions (see pages 147–8). If you are writing on behalf of a group or an organization, you can use the pronoun *we*, which is less intrusive than awkward passive constructions; if you are writing as an individual, however, you don't have that option. If this is the case, try to recast the sentence in order to keep an active verb while avoiding *I*:

✗ The purchasing system <u>has been found</u> to increase the duplication of forms.

✗ <u>I found</u> that the purchasing system increases the duplication of forms.

✓ The purchasing system <u>increases</u> the duplication of forms.

If you can't make this sort of revision, you are better to use the occasional *I* than to strangle your meaning in a convoluted *I*-less sentence. In any case, don't substitute *the writer* or *the researcher* for *I*.

Be specific

Although you don't have to give complete descriptive details for every fact you report, you should be as precise as possible when referring to people, places, times, and amounts—especially if you think the information might be disputed. Instead of saying

> Some time last month the president contacted one of the managers and learned that some of the computers were down.

say

> On 25 May, the president, Nathalie Charbonneau, spoke to the manager of information systems, Emma Irvin, and learned that six computers could not access the PeopleSoft database.

Take care also to be specific in defining key terms. Precision is particularly important in the case of words such as *reliable*, which may have a special technical meaning to some people but a more general one to others. To avoid confusion you must make sure that your readers know exactly how you are using such terms.

Finally, remember that by being specific you will make your writing not only clearer but more interesting as well: concrete language is lively language.

Use headings to tell the story

A report, unlike an essay, should use headings to distinguish the various sections. A heading or subheading may simply indicate the topic of each section—for example, *Discussion of Findings*—but it will be much more effective if it summarizes the most important point. Headings that "tell the story" enable the reader to find the key points in your report at a glance. For example, a heading such as *Reduced Inventories* or *Inconsistent Layoff Policies* gives the reader more information than *Inventories* or *Layoffs*. The outline for the report on network servers (pages 62–3) provides a fuller illustration.

Number each section

Numbering helps to indicate each section's relative importance. Here are the three basic systems:

Roman numeral	Alphanumeric	Decimal
I	A.	1.0
A.	1.	1.1
1.	a.	1.11
2.	b.	1.12
B.	2.	1.2
II	B.	2.0

Increasingly, technical reports are using the decimal system. Whichever method you choose, be sure to use equivalent symbols for sections of equivalent importance.

List information

Whenever you can simplify your material by listing it, do so. A list, like a heading, is an aid to quick understanding. As a guideline, list any sequence of three items or more. If you will be referring to the items in the list later, number each one; otherwise you may simply use a dash (—) or a bullet (•).

Use illustrations

Tables, graphs, and other illustrations—especially those that analyze a quantity of data—are common and useful in business reports. Such visual aids can help the reader to quickly grasp information that would take many words to explain. Visual aids allow you to summarize information without repeating what you have said in words. (See Chapter 6 for guidelines on creating effective illustrations.)

When trying to decide where in the report to include illustrations, you must determine the importance of the information you are trying to present. If a graph or table contains supplementary information, you should place it in an appendix; if the information is essential, you should try to position the graphic next to the relevant discussion in the text. If you must place an illustration somewhere far from the relevant text, make sure that you number and label it and that in the text you refer both to the illustration itself and to the point it makes: "As Figure 2 shows, costs have decreased for each of the last five years."

Create visual appeal

Here are some other suggestions for producing a report that is appealing to the eye as well as the mind:

- Leave a generous amount of space around the text to create a pleasing impression; wide margins and spaces between sections will help to break up an imposing mass of type.
- Make headings stand out by using bold, italics, or upper case.
- Use different alignment and font sizes for different levels of headings. Systems for formatting headings vary, but this is a common one:

PRIMARY HEADING
CENTRED, UPPERCASE, 14-POINT

Secondary Heading at Left Margin

The heading is 13-point bold type. The initial letter of the first and other important words is in uppercase, and the text begins on a new line.

Third-level heading. The heading is in 12-point italics and may be indented; only the first letter of the first word is in uppercase. The text follows on the same line.

No matter what style you decide on, remember that the essential ingredients for headings with visual appeal are clarity and consistency.

Using Illustrations

In this chapter, we will examine

- guidelines for using visual aids effectively;
- the type of information best represented in a table; and
- the appropriate use of line, bar, and pie charts.

Introduction

People are accustomed to seeing and interpreting visual representations of ideas. From international traffic symbols to corporate logos, visual symbols and illustrations are part of our everyday lives. Our increasing reliance on the visual may result in part from the influence of television and the Internet. It also reflects the multicultural nature of our society and the need to communicate ideas quickly with images and symbols that transcend linguistic and cultural barriers. Most current computer programs operate on graphical interfaces that use images instead of text. The visual representation of information can indeed be worth a thousand words: it allows us to *see* the point.

Especially when writing reports, consider whether you can display some of your information with graphics rather than text. Computer programs make it easy to create, format, and annotate tables, charts, and diagrams that illustrate important points in your essay or report. Here are a few basic guidelines for using visual aids effectively:

- Information in an illustration should expand on or complement information in the text, not simply duplicate it.
- Simple illustrations are better than cluttered ones. The easier it is for the reader to grasp the information quickly and accurately, the better.
- As in report headings and subheadings, try to make the title of the visual reflect the point of the illustration, not just the topic. When this is

not possible, at least be specific about the content. For example, a title such as *April Decline in Employment* or *Ontario Job Market: Monthly Employment Figures* is better than *Employment Figures.*

- Refer to every illustration in the text, explaining why it is there or what it shows. If you have several illustrations, number each one so that you can refer to it by number in the discussion:

    . . . (see Figure 1).
    As Figure 1 shows, . . .

Tables

A table can convey a large amount of information, both numerical and textual, without losing detail. If you are giving specific information in numerical form, a table allows you to show precise data more clearly than a graph or chart does. It is the sensible choice for data too detailed or too complex to be clearly illustrated in a chart, for example, when small differences in sales figures are critical, or when some or all of the information is text based. Table 6.1 illustrates the type of information that is best represented in a table.

Table 6.1 Professional development activity, 2014

Department	Participants	Rate of Participation	Hours	Budget	Report
Human Resources	27	73%	16	$9500	Y
Advertising and Public Relations	23	62%	8	$4500	Y
Sales	45	93%	12	$2800	Y
Research	14	54%	14	$2100	N
Finance	17	85%	25	$1850	Y

Charts

Although they aren't quite as precise as tables, charts can dramatize information more effectively and are easier for the reader to grasp. Programs such as Microsoft Office offer a wide range of chart types, but here are three of the most common:

Line charts

A *line chart* (see Figure 6.1) shows change over a period of time; it's often used to point out trends or fluctuations, as in a sales report. In devising a line chart, put quantities on the vertical axis and time values on the horizontal axis. Try to shape the dimensions of the graph to give the most accurate impression of the extent of change. Never distort your graph to emphasize a point—for instance, by shortening the horizontal axis and lengthening the vertical axis to make a gradual rise look more dramatic. Doing so will only reduce your credibility and cause your reader to question the reliability of your information and the validity of your arguments.

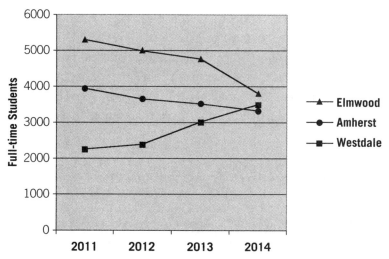

Figure 6.1   Tri-campus enrollment figures, 2011–2014

Bar charts

A *bar chart* is used to compare elements at fixed points in time. You might use a bar chart to show the profits made by each department in a company in a particular year or the changes in a company's sales from one year to the next. The bars can be horizontal or vertical, depending on the range of data, and they can be segmented (stacked) to show different parts of the whole. For example, a bar representing a company's sales for a given year could be segmented to show what part of the total is domestic sales and what part is foreign sales. Bars can also be clustered or grouped to compare one category with another, as in Figure 6.2.

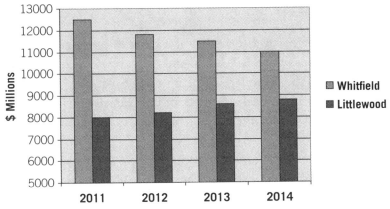

Figure 6.2 Investment performance: Whitfield and Littlewood, 2011–2014

Pie charts

A *pie chart* is used to emphasize proportions—to draw attention to the relative size of the parts that make up a whole. For example, it can provide a quick visual comparison of individual department sales as a proportion of total sales. With a pie chart you can also show percentages and explode one piece of the pie for emphasis, as in Figure 6.3.

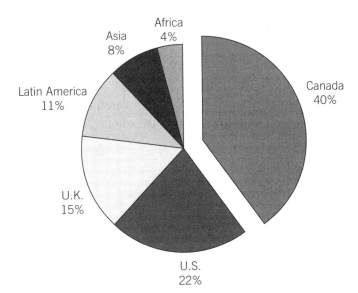

Figure 6.3 International students at Millbrook College, Winter 2014

Tables or Charts?

When deciding whether to use a table or a chart to present your data, you must always consider which will be the most effective in getting your point across. Tables have the advantage of being more exact than charts because they provide precise numerical information. They can also include text as well as numerical data. On the other hand, charts often give a more compelling impression of the overall pattern of results.

In general, a table is a good choice if you have several sets of numbers that could get buried if you just listed them in the text. However, if you have statistics for a number of conditions that vary systematically, a chart is the best way to illustrate the information. Sometimes, the choice between a table and a chart comes down to nothing more than personal style or preference.

Two Dangers in Using Illustrations

- Computer programs offer a wide range of features and options for tables and charts. These elements can add visual impact and even drama to your written material, but they do make it tempting to add so much detail that you obscure the facts. Be sure that the designs you create are not too elaborate for your purpose. Visuals are meant not to dazzle but to make it easier for the reader to understand.
- Any illustration, even if it is created on a computer, can distort information. For instance, the slope of a graph line can be made to look steep or shallow, even with the same data; trend lines can begin at a time that omits unfavourable periods. Although line and bar charts are the most susceptible to distortion, the shapes and proportions of other diagrams can also give a false picture. Be careful to present as accurate a picture as possible so that your illustrations reinforce the credibility of your words.

Documenting Sources

In this chapter, we will examine

- strategies for incorporating quoted material into an essay;
- current guidelines for MLA, APA, Chicago, and CSE styles of documentation; and
- formats for writing annotated bibliographies.

Introduction

Much of the writing you do will require you to consult secondary sources to become familiar with current research and to find support for your ideas. It's essential to acknowledge those sources, not only when you quote directly from them but also when you restate, in your own words, arguments or ideas taken from them. If you don't acknowledge your sources you're allowing your reader to assume that the words, ideas, or thoughts are yours; in other words, you're plagiarizing, and the penalties can be severe.

The purpose of documentation is not only to avoid charges of plagiarism but also to show the body of knowledge that your work is building on. Academic writing is based on the premise that researchers are not working in a vacuum but are indebted to those scholars who came before them. By documenting your sources, you are showing that you understand this concept and are ready to make your own contribution to the body of knowledge in your field.

Using Quotations

Judicious use of quotations can add authority to your writing as well as help you avoid charges of plagiarism, but you must use quotations with care. Never quote a passage just because it sounds impressive; be sure that it really adds to your discussion, either by expressing an idea with special force or cogency or by giving substance to a debatable point. The following are some guidelines for incorporating quotations in your work:

1. Avoid incorporating quotations as complete sentences in your text; instead, integrate quotations into your own prose. Be sure that a quotation makes sense in the context of your discussion and fits grammatically into a sentence:

    ✗ Whether Bill Gates was a visionary is debatable. "640 K ought to be enough for anybody" was soon considered laughable.

    ✓ Whether Bill Gates was a visionary is debatable. His 1981 prediction that "640 K ought to be enough for anybody" was soon considered laughable.

2. Short quotations should be included as part of your text, enclosed in quotation marks. Longer quotations should be set as a block of freestanding text. Generally, quotations of a certain number of lines (in your document) or words are integrated while quotations that exceed these parameters are formatted as block quotations. Style guides differ with regard to the lengths appropriate to integrated and block quotations as well as the formatting requirements for each, so be sure to consult the style guide appropriate to your discipline.

3. Be accurate. Reproduce the exact wording, punctuation, and spelling of the original, including any errors or irregularities (like text in italics or bold or unusual word or line spacing in verse). You can acknowledge a typo or mistake in the original by inserting the Latin word *sic* in square brackets (see page 168) within the quotation or in parentheses after the quotation. If you want to italicize part of the quotation for emphasis, add "my emphasis" or "emphasis added" in square brackets within the quotation or in parentheses after the quotation. If you want to insert an explanatory comment of your own into a quotation, enclose your words in square brackets:

    "At private meetings, two councillors [Smith and Robertson] strenuously objected to the proposal."

4. If you want to omit something from the original, use ellipsis marks; see page 175 for details.

Documenting Your Sources

There are many systems of documentation and the one you use will depend on the subject you are writing about as well as the preference of your instructor, your department, or your employer. Begin by finding out if there is a preferred documentation style and set of guidelines for its use. If there isn't, you should consider following one of the four most common systems of documentation described below. Remember, though, that style guides are constantly undergoing revision, especially with the wealth of online information currently available. It's always safest to check the latest edition of the relevant manual or the appropriate website to be sure that you have the most up-to-date information available.

Note also that the latest version of your word-processing software automatically formats endnotes, footnotes, and citations as well as bibliographies and lists of works cited according to MLA, APA, and Chicago styles. It's worth your while becoming familiar with these features as they are fast and accurate and can save you a great deal of time and effort.

MLA Style

The *MLA Handbook*, published by the Modern Language Association, is commonly referred to for guidance in documenting sources in the humanities. The MLA style uses in-text citations, which give the page number or, when necessary, the author's last name and the page number in parentheses after a paraphrase of or quotation from the original source. Complete bibliographical information is then given in an alphabetical list, titled *Works Cited*, on a separate page at the end of the essay or report.

The following examples illustrate some of the most common types of references as they would appear in citations and in the *Works Cited* list. If you don't see what you're looking for, consult the *MLA Handbook for Writers of Research Papers* (7th ed., 2009).

Note that books and journals or anything else published as a large or independent volume (such as a magazine or newspaper) must be italicized (for instance, *Journal of Contemporary History*) while anything that is part of a larger work or collection (such as an article, essay, poem, or short story) is not italicized and is instead enclosed in quotation marks with every significant word in the title capitalized (for instance, "Treacherous Allies: The Cold War in East Asia and American Postwar Anxiety").

Quotations

If a quotation from a prose work is four lines or fewer, enclose it in quotation marks and integrate it into your text. Note that quotation marks within the original are changed to single quotation marks within the quotation. Note also that in integrated quotations, your punctuation to continue or conclude the sentence comes *after* the parenthetical citation.

> Throughout *Black White and Jewish*, Rebecca Walker explores the way in which her family's legitimacy is questioned as soon as her family is formed: "'Correct?' it [a note on her birth certificate] says. 'Correct?' a faceless questioner wants to know. Is this union, this marriage, and especially this offspring, correct?" (13).

If the quotation is more than four lines in your document, do not enclose it in quotation marks; instead, include it as a freestanding block of text, indented one inch from the left margin only. Note that in block quotations, double quotation marks within the original are not changed to single quotation marks. Note also that in block quotations, the parenthetical citation comes after the period and is not followed by any punctuation:

> When her father tells her the story of her birth, Walker recognizes that her family is incomprehensible in the segregated South:
>
>> A nurse walks into Mama's room, my birth certificate in hand. At first glance, all of the information seems straightforward enough: mother, father, address, and so on. But next to boxes labelled "Mother's Race" and "Father's Race," which read Negro and Caucasian, there is a curious note tucked into the margin. "Correct?" it says. "Correct?" a faceless questioner wants to know. Is this union, this marriage, and especially this offspring, correct? (12–13)

It is as much her parents' love and in particular her white father's devotion to her black mother and to their baby as it is Walker herself that is being questioned in the Mississippi hospital.

No font style or size change is required in either integrated or block quotations. Your document should be entirely double-spaced including all quotations and the *Works Cited* list.

In-text citations

Book or article with one author

Put in parentheses (round brackets) only the information needed to identify a source clearly—usually the author's (or editor's) last name. If you're referring to a specific part of the source, also include the page number:

> This type of musical parody is often "conservative in impulse" (Hutcheon 92).

Place the parenthetical reference where a pause would naturally occur, preferably at the end of the sentence or clause it documents. Note that there is no punctuation between the author's name and the page number.

If the author's name is already given in the text, put in parentheses only the page number of the reference:

> In fact, Hutcheon argues that this type of musical parody is often "conservative in impulse" (92).

If you are referencing an entire work, try to include the author's (or editor's) name in the text:

> In *A Theory of Parody*, Linda Hutcheon examines a range of contemporary art forms.

Book or article with more than one author

If the work has two or three authors, include all of the names in the citation:

> The same argument was applied to the universities (Matthews and Steele 50–62).

If the work has four or more authors, either use only the first author's last name and "et al." or provide all of the last names. Use the same form in the *Works Cited* section:

> The result, some claim, is "cultural suicide" (Jones et al. 42).

or

> However, another study disagrees with this finding (Collins, Collom, Mills, Pecan, and Stuart 74).

Literary works

Some texts, especially classical ones, are conventionally cited by section or chapter. Poetry should always be referenced by line numbers. Referencing drama will depend on the conventions the playwright has used. For much of contemporary drama, page numbers will suffice; however, formally structured plays (with act, scene, and line numbers) must be cited by act, scene, and line(s) in that order, all in arabic numerals and separated by periods.

> In *A Midsummer Night's Dream*, we find a different perspective on the nature of love: "The lunatic, the lover and the poet / Are of imagination all compact" (5.1.7–8).

When quoting multiple lines of poetry or other verse (in an integrated quotation), insert a forward slash between the lines with a space on either side (/) as in the example above. Block quotations should reproduce the line breaks of the original:

> In *A Midsummer Night's Dream*, we find a different perspective on the nature of love:
>
>> Lovers and madmen have such seething brains,
>> Such shaping fantasies, that apprehend
>> More than cool reason ever comprehends.
>> The lunatic, the lover and the poet
>> Are of imagination all compact. (5.1.4–8)

Three lines of verse or fewer can be formatted as an integrated quotation using slashes to separate lines; four or more lines of verse should be offset as a block quotation. Dialogue in drama should be offset as a block quotation with each speaker indented one inch from the left (as usual); the name of the character should be capitalized in its entirety and followed by a period. Each subsequent line of that character's speech should be indented an additional quarter inch. This format should be repeated with each shift in speaker. Stage directions are part of the text and should be quoted accordingly.

> In Andrew Moodie's *Riot*, a group of roommates discusses the anti-black racism of the U.S. in the wake of the Rodney King beating:
>
> > ALEX. . . . the way they treated Rodney King has been police procedure, in America, for quite some time. And if it wasn't for that video tape, we wouldn't even be talking about it.
> > EFFIE. As a matter of fact, it took a long time for the video to even make it into the news. A lot of stations refused to play it at first.
> > GRACE. Shhh. They're playing the video again.
> >
> > *They watch together in silence for a while. They react to the video.* (23)

Book or article with no known or declared author

If the work has no known or listed author, give the title or the beginning of it, using italics in the case of a book and quotation marks in the case of an article (as usual):

> In ferociously anti-union editorials, Laurier argued that Quebec should sever its ties with Britain ("A Rebel" 68).

Book or article with a group or corporate author

If you are citing a document prepared by a corporate author or a government agency, give the name of the organization. In a parenthetical citation, omit any definite or indefinite article that appears at the beginning of the group's name.

However, it is often clearer to include the organization's full name in your sentence rather than in your citation:

> Until a correction appeared on the website, Canada Post Corporation showed the abbreviation for both Nunavut and Northwest Territories as "NT" (14).

Two or more works by the same author

If you need to refer to more than one work written by the same author, use a shortened version of the appropriate title with each citation. Note that in the citation the author's last name is followed by a comma and then the abbreviated title and page number:

> It's useful to think of business communication as presenting a problem for which there may be no single solution (Northey, *Impact* 25).

If the author's name and the title appear in the text, indicate only the page number(s) in parentheses. If the author's name appears in the text, include only the title and page number(s) in parentheses. Note that the citation includes no punctuation:

> Northey suggests that it's useful to think of business communication as a problem for which there may be no single solution (*Impact* 25).

Electronic sources

In-text citations for electronic sources use the same formatting principles outlined above for print sources. However, since many electronic sources do not have page numbers, you may have to cite a paragraph or section number instead:

> ("Stocks," sec. 2)

> (Douglas, pars. 12–15)

If your source has no page, section, or paragraph numbers, it is preferable to include the name of the author or title in the text.

Works cited

Your list of works cited should contain only those works you have actually referred to in the text; do not include works that you consulted but did not cite directly in your essay. The following are some formatting guidelines, followed by examples of common entries in a *Works Cited* list. If the kind of source you are using isn't shown in any of the examples here, consult the *MLA Handbook*.

- Begin your *Works Cited* section on a separate page but continue the page numbering from the last page of your essay.
- Double-space the entire list, both between and within entries and between the title and the first entry.
- Do not number entries, but list them alphabetically by the author's or editor's surname. If no author is given, begin with the first significant word in the title.
- Format with hanging indents: begin each bibliographic entry at the margin and indent any subsequent line half an inch. It is easiest, and avoids formatting errors, to simply set your paragraph indentation style as "hanging" in the *Works Cited* section of your document.
- Separate the main divisions with periods.

Note that short forms are always preferable. For instance, entries need not include long versions of publishers' names, so Plume Books is simply "Plume," Random House Inc. is "Random House," and W. W. Norton & Co. is "Norton" in a *Works Cited* list. Similarly, the words *university* and *press* are shortened to the letters *U* and *P* when the publisher is a university press, so Oxford University Press is "Oxford UP" and University of Toronto Press is "U of Toronto P." Note also that if a book is published by a publisher's "imprint," the imprint is stated first followed by a hyphen and the publisher: for instance, "Perennial-Harper."

Book with one author
The basic entry provides the author's last and first names followed by the title of the text, the city of publication, the publisher, the year of publication, and the text's medium:

Brand, Dionne. *What We All Long For*. Toronto: Knopf, 2005. Print.

Frequently, literature students will be using recent reprints of texts published previously. It is advisable to observe the original date of publication within the *Works Cited* entry; this is done simply by adding the original year of publication after the title:

> Brontë, Charlotte. *Jane Eyre*. 1847. New York: Penguin, 2006. Print.

Book with more than one author

If a book you have cited was written by two or three authors, list all of the authors in the order in which they appear on the title page, separated with commas, with only the first author's name inverted:

> Ray, Paul H., and Sherry Ruth Anderson. *The Cultural Creatives: How 50 Million People Are Changing the World*. New York: Broadway, 2001. Print.

If the book has four or more authors, you may either list all the names in full in the order in which they appear on the title page, with only the first author's name inverted, or give only the first author's name, inverted, followed by a comma and "et al.":

> Scholes, Dieter, et al. *Prosody and Poetics: An Introduction*. New York: Hudson, 1999. Print.

Two or more books by the same author

Entries for two or more books by the same author are arranged alphabetically by the first significant word in the title. List the author's name in the first entry only; in subsequent entries, use three hyphens in place of the author's name:

> Macmillan, Margaret. *Paris 1919: Six Months That Changed the World*. New York: Random House, 2003. Print.
>
> ---. *The War That Ended Peace*. New York: Random House, 2013. Print.

Book with a group or corporate author

Cite the book by the corporate author, which may be a commission, an association, or a committee, omitting any initial article such as "A," "An," or "The":

> Boston Women's Health Book Collective. *Our Bodies, Ourselves*. New York: Touchstone, 2011. Print.

Book with an editor

> King, J. E., ed. *The Elgar Companion to Post Keynesian Economics.* Northhampton: Elgar, 2003. Print.

If you are listing a book with more than one editor, follow the guidelines given above for a book with more than one author, listing the editors' names followed by "eds."

An edition or volume of a book
If you are using a textbook or other volume that is updated regularly in new, revised editions, provide the edition after the title:

> Perry, John, Michael Bratman, and John Martin Fischer, eds. *Introduction to Philosophy: Classical and Contemporary Readings.* 5th ed. New York: Oxford UP, 2010. Print.

To list one volume of a multi-volume work, provide the volume number after the edition:

> Baym, Nina, et al., eds. *The Norton Anthology of American Literature.* 8th ed. Vol. A. New York: W. W. Norton, 2011. Print.

Book with a translator
List the text under the author's name. Only in cases where the translation or translator is the focus of your discussion should the text be listed by the translator's name.

> Grass, Günter. *The Tin Drum.* Trans. Ralph Manheim. New York: Vintage, 1962. Print.

> Mitchell, Breon, trans. *The Tin Drum.* By Günter Grass. Boston: Mariner, 2010. Print.

Selection in an edited book
A text reproduced in an anthology or a chapter in an edited volume should be listed by the author of the work, not the editor of the compilation. Make sure to provide inclusive page numbers for the entire piece, not just for the material you used. The original year of publication may be

provided after an anthologized selection. Often, anthologies will include excerpts from long works; in these cases, you may state "Excerpt from" before the title. Remember that titles of excerpts from or reproductions of texts originally published as books must be italicized (as in the Chopin example below).

Adah, Anthony. "On the Field of Battle: First Nations Women Documentary Filmmakers." *The Gendered Screen: Canadian Women Filmmakers*. Ed. Brenda Austin-Smith and George Melnyk. Waterloo: Wilfrid Laurier UP, 2010. 165–83. Print.

Chopin, Kate. *The Awakening*. 1899. *Heath Anthology of American Literature*. Ed. Paul Lauter et al. 5th ed. Vol. E. Boston: Houghton Mifflin, 2006. 363–453. Print.

Article in a journal

When listing a journal article, give the author, the title of the article, the journal title, the volume number, the issue number if available, the year of publication, and the inclusive page numbers. Omit introductory definite and indefinite articles in the journal title.

Belsey, Catherine. "Shakespeare's Sad Tale for Winter: *Hamlet* and the Tradition of Fireside Ghost Stories." *Shakespeare Quarterly* 61.1 (2010): 1–27. Print.

Lindsay, Peter. "Overcoming False Dichotomies: Mill, Marx and the Welfare State." *History of Political Thought* 4 (2000): 657–81. Print.

Article in a magazine

Include the date shown on the issue, abbreviating all months except for May, June, and July. Do not give volume or issue numbers.

Ferguson, Sue, and D'arcy Jenish. "A Rebel at Heart?" *Maclean's* 1 July 2001: 68–69. Print.

Sumner, Wayne. "The Morgentaler Effect." *Walrus* Jan.–Feb. 2011: 44–50. Print.

Article in a newspaper

The guidelines for listing a newspaper article are similar to those for listing a magazine, except that the page number sometimes includes a letter identifying the section of the newspaper in which the article is found:

> Renzetti, Elizabeth. "So Much Paper, So Little Action." *Globe and Mail* 24 Mar. 2014: A13. Print.

Not all newspaper references are this straightforward. Bear in mind the following guidelines:

- As with journals and magazines, omit introductory articles in the title of the newspaper.
- If the city of publication is not included in the name of a locally published newspaper, add it in square brackets after the title: *Chronicle Herald* [Halifax]. You do not need to add the city of publication for nationally published newspapers: *Globe and Mail.*
- When an article has no listed author, begin the entry with the article title.
- If the newspaper section is identified by a number rather than a letter, use "sec." followed by the section number followed by a colon and the page number; separate this information from the date with a comma.
- In the case of a particular edition used—such as an early or late edition or one published in a particular location—the edition information follows the date and a comma and is itself followed by a colon and the page number.
- When an article is continued on a page that is not the next consecutive page, the page number is followed by a plus sign (+) and a period:

> Kopun, Francine. "The Healing Lens." *Toronto Star* 17 May 2008: D1+. Print.

Lecture, speech, address, or reading

Give the speaker's name, the title in quotation marks, the meeting and sponsoring organization if applicable, the location, the date, and an appropriate medium label:

> Millar, Edythe. "Theories of Third-Wave Feminism." York University, Toronto. 28 Feb. 2011. Lecture.

Electronic sources

Because of the wide variety and continued development of new electronic resources, citing them can be difficult. Often, scholars must improvise based on established bibliographic rules. The following information is usually included and in this order:

- author
- title of the work, italicized if the work is independent, in roman type and quotation marks if it's part of a larger work
- title of the website (italicized)
- version or edition
- publisher of the website
- date of publication
- medium (Web)
- date of access

As you navigate the use of electronic resources in your work and improvise on style requirements for new resources, bear in mind the following guidelines:

- Whenever possible, begin each *Works Cited* entry with the name of the author, compiler, director, editor, narrator, performer, or translator of the work and identify his or her role whenever necessary. If no such person is evident, begin your entry with the title.
- As with print resources, works that are independent must be italicized and those that are part of larger works must be enclosed in quotation marks instead. The names of whole websites should be italicized, for instance, while a webpage or document on the website should be enclosed in quotation marks.
- The date the information was published online or last updated should be provided in your entry between the publisher and the medium. If no date is provided, state "n.d."
- The publisher or sponsor of the site should be listed after the name of the website. If no publisher or sponsor is evident, state "N.p."
- Always include the medium (Web) and your date of access, in that order.

Referencing online resources is sometimes complicated by the temporary and changing nature of how and what information is available on the Internet.

Generally, URLs are excluded because they are so unstable and cumbersome; however, when you anticipate your reader will not be able to find the resource you have cited or when an instructor requires it, provide the URL at the end of your entry enclosed in angle brackets. When a URL must be divided across multiple lines in your document, ensure that the line break occurs after a slash. Do not introduce any punctuation (such as a hyphen at a line break or period at the end) into the URL itself. Complete your entry with a period outside the bracket. If you choose to provide a URL, provide the complete URL (including "http:// ") for the specific work you are citing.

> *Civil Rights in Mississippi Digital Archive.* U of Southern Mississippi Lib., n.d. Web. 25 Mar. 2014. <http://digilib.usm.edu/crmda.php>.

> Minnis, Jack. "A Chronology of Violence and Intimidation in Mississippi Since 1961." *Civil Rights in Mississippi Digital Archive.* U of Southern Mississippi Lib., n.d. Web. 20 Mar. 2014. <http://digilib.usm.edu/cdm4/document.php?CISOROOT=/manu&CISOPTR=3118&REC=2>.

Website

When referencing an entire website, list the entry by the website name and include the publisher, date of publication (if available), medium, and date of access.

> *The Glen Gould Archive.* Library and Archives Canada, 7 Jan. 2004. Web. 20 Feb. 2014.

> *The Modern American Poetry Site.* U of Illinois, 1999. Web. 12 Apr. 2014.

Article in an online journal

List an article from an online scholarly journal the same way as you would an article from a print scholarly journal, changing the medium of publication (to Web) and adding the date of access at the end of your entry. If the online journal does not provide "page" numbers, state "n. pag." Online journals may not follow conventional pagination formatting, so you may need to improvise appropriately; for instance, in the Truman example below, the online journal numbers each article (1) and the sections within each article (1–37), so the *Works Cited* lists 1.1–37 as the article's pagination. Unlike many other Web resources, online scholarly journals tend to offer consistent and somewhat thorough publication information since academics and researchers require such details.

Gordon, Jon F. "Means and Motives: The Mystification of Mountaineering Discourse." *Postcolonial Text* 2.4 (2006): n. pag. Web. 2 June 2009.

Kelly, Jennifer R. "Black Canadian Studies: A Move Towards Diasporan Literacy." *New Dawn* 1.1 (2009): 88–94. Web. 3 May 2010.

Truman, James C. W. "The Body in Pain in Early Modern England." *Early Modern Literary Studies* 14.3 (2009): 1.1–37. Web. 18 Jan. 2011.

Magazine or newspaper article published online

Provide the author's name and the article title as usual. Then provide the website name italicized, followed by the publisher (often of the same name or similar name) without italics as well as the date of publication. Conclude your entry with the medium and date of access.

Adler, Ben. "Conservatives Make Inaccurate Arguments against Gun Control." *Newsweek*. Newsweek, 18 Jan. 2011. Web. 19 Jan. 2011.

Norton-Taylor, Richard. "EU Criticised for 'Complicity' in CIA Rendition Programmes." *Guardian.co.uk*. Guardian News and Media, 16 Nov. 2010. Web. 21 Jan. 2011.

Article from a Web magazine

References to articles from Web magazines follow the same format as other Web resources and list the author, article title, magazine title, publisher or sponsor, date of publication, medium, and date of access.

Lemonick, Michael. "Can We Trust Climate Models? Increasingly, the Answer Is 'Yes'." *Yale Environment 360*. Yale School of Forestry and Environmental Studies, 18 Jan. 2011. Web. 19 Jan. 2011.

Work from a database

For articles from online databases such as JSTOR or ProQuest, reference as for print sources, adding the title of the database in italics, the medium of access, and the date of access:

Serpell, C. Namwali. "Mutual Exclusion, Oscillation, and Ethical Projection in *The Crying of Lot 49* and *The Turn of the Screw*." *Narrative* 16.3 (2008): 223–55. *Project Muse*. Web. 7 July 2010.

Non-periodical publication online

The majority of works online are non-periodical (i.e., not published at regular intervals). This category is broad and can include websites sponsored by news organizations, broadcasters, institutions, professional organizations, and countless other groups or individuals.

If a website is organized by page, paragraph, or section, give the relevant number(s) preceded by an appropriate abbreviation, such as "par.," "pars.," or "sec." Where no numbering system is used, do not count pages or paragraphs, and omit any specific reference to pagination.

Works Cited entries for non-periodical online publications follow the same protocol as do periodical online entries and include the same information with the appropriate alterations and additions depending on the type of resource you are referencing. Remember that webpages and articles are enclosed in quotation marks while websites themselves are italicized. The following are examples of *Works Cited* entries for general non-periodical online publications:

> Brooks, Gwendolyn, narr. "We Real Cool." By Brooks. *Poets.org*. Academy of American Poets, 1997. Web. 14 Feb. 2014.
>
> "Film Noir." *Wikipedia*. Wikipedia Foundation, n.d. Web. 12 June 2014.
>
> Miner, Mike. "Searchlight 2014: The Hunt for Canada's Best New Artist." *CBC.ca*. CBC/Radio-Canada, 10 Mar. 2014. Web. 24 Mar. 2014.

Scanned book

If the non-periodical work also appears in print, for example a scanned book, list the bibliographic information for the print publication and add the title of the website, the medium of publication, and the date of access.

> World Bank. *Historic Cities and Sacred Sites: Cultural Roots and Urban Futures*. Washington: World Bank, 2012. *Google Books*. Web. 8 Apr. 2014.

E-mail

List an e-mail by the author of the message, followed by the subject line in quotation marks. Identify to whom the message was sent, the date the message was sent, and the medium.

> Mukherjee, Gurjit. "Re: National Gallery Exhibit." Message to Midori Okada. 15 Nov. 2014. E-mail.

Blog

> Rohter, Larry. "Which Jazz Greats Were Left Off the Blue Note 100?" *ArtsBeat: The Culture at Large*. New York Times, 24 Mar. 2014. Web. 31 Mar. 2014.

Discussion list

> Alkalimat, Abdul. "How America Built the Racial Wealth Gap." *H-Afro-Am Discussion Logs*. H-Net, 9 Apr. 2013. Web. 25 Mar. 2014.

APA Style

The American Psychological Association system of documentation is the one most commonly used in the social sciences, business, and nursing. Like the MLA style, the APA system uses parenthetical citations within the text keyed to a list of references at the end. Some examples are listed below.

For more detailed information, consult the *Publication Manual of the American Psychological Association* (6th ed., 2010) as well as *APA Style Guide to Electronic References* (2012) or visit the APA website (apastyle.apa.org).

Quotations

If a quotation from a prose work is fewer than 40 words, enclose it in quotation marks and integrate it into your text. Note that quotation marks within the original are changed to single quotation marks within the quotation. Note also that in integrated quotations, your punctuation to continue or conclude the sentence comes after the parenthetical citation. If the quotation is 40 or more words, do not enclose it in quotation marks; instead, include it as a free-standing block of text, double-spaced and indented about a half inch from the left margin only. Note that in block quotations, double quotation marks within the original are not changed within the quotation. Note also that in block quotations, the parenthetical citation comes after the period and is not followed by any punctuation.

In-text citations
Book or article with one author
If the author's name is given in the text, cite only the year of publication in parentheses. Otherwise, give both the author's surname and the year:

Helmsteadt (2013) made a significant contribution to the climate change debate.

The latest statistical analysis (Christensen, 2014) disproved government statements.

Book or article with more than one author
If the work you are citing has two authors, include the surnames of each author every time you cite the reference in the text. The APA uses an ampersand (&) when the names are in parentheses but "and" in the text:

> Initial research showed that neonates did not distinguish between small frequency differences (Leventhal & Lipsitt, 1964). However, Morrongiello and Clifton (1984) later discovered that neonates orient better to high- than to low-frequency sounds.

If there are three, four, or five authors, cite the surnames of each author when the reference first occurs and afterwards cite only the first author, followed by "et al.":

> Krassanakis, Filippakopoulou, and Nakos (2014) studied eye movements. . . . Research included the development of a new toolbox for post experimental eye movement analysis (Krassanakis et al., 2014).

If the work you are citing has six or more authors, cite only the surname of the first author followed by "et al."

Book or article with a group or corporate author
The names of corporations, associations, and government agencies serving as authors are usually given in full each time they appear. Some group authors may be given in full the first time and abbreviated in subsequent citations if this provides the reader with enough information to easily locate the entry in the reference list. For parenthetical citations, include the abbreviation in brackets the first time the source is cited; in subsequent citations use only the abbreviation:

> One study found that workers in western provinces had a higher risk of work injuries compared with Ontario workers (Institute for Work & Health

[IWH], 2013). . . . The same study concluded that future research is required to identify the provincial determinants for workplace injuries (IWH, 2013).

Article with no known or declared author
If the work you are referencing has no known or declared author, cite the first few words of the title as well as the year:

Researchers found that it was not uncommon for seniors to be taking as many as 10 pills a day ("Our Alarming Culture," 2013).

In this case, the full title of the article is "Our Alarming Culture of Pill People and Future Trends in Healthcare."

Specific parts of a source
If you are referring to a particular part of a source, you must indicate the page, chapter, figure, table, or equation. Always give page numbers for quotations:

(Thompson, 2013, p. 299)

(Bayly & Peterson, 2014, pp. 2601–2602)

(Stenson, 2013, Chapter 2)

Note that the APA prefaces page numbers with "p." for a single page and "pp." for multiple pages.

Electronic sources
In-text citations for electronic sources use the same formatting principles outlined above for print sources, with the following exceptions. If your particular source is not included here, visit the APA Style blog (blog.apastyle.org) for advice, or consult the *APA Style Guide to Electronic References*.

- If your source has no page numbers, use the paragraph number if one is available, preceded by the abbreviation "para.":

    (Edson, 2014, para. 10)

- If sections, pages, and paragraphs are not numbered, cite the heading and the number of the paragraph following it to direct the reader to the specific location you are referring to:

(Black, 2013, Introduction, para. 6)

References

Entries in an APA *References* section are similar to those in an MLA *Works Cited* list with the following exceptions:

- Entries begin with the author's surname, followed by his or her initials; full given names are not used.
- For works with multiple authors, all names are reversed; the name of the last author is preceded by an ampersand (&) rather than "and."
- The date of publication appears immediately after the authors' names.
- Entries for different works by the same author are listed chronologically. Two or more works by the same author with the same publication date are arranged alphabetically by title.
- For titles of books and articles, only proper nouns and the first word of the title and of the subtitle if there is one are capitalized.
- Titles of articles or selections in books are not enclosed in quotation marks.

Book with one author

Klein, N. (2009). *No logo: 10th anniversary edition*. Toronto, Canada: Vintage.

Book with more than one author

Doty, D. I., & Pincus, M. (2001). *Publicity and public relations* (2nd ed.). New York, NY: Barron's.

For books with eight or more authors, list only the first six followed by three ellipses and the last author's name.

Book with a group or corporate author

American Medical Association. (2007). *Guides to the evaluation of permanent impairment* (6th ed.). Chicago, IL: Author.

Book with an editor

> Bennett, D., & Brown, R. (Eds.). (2010). *An anthology of Canadian literature in English* (3rd ed.). Don Mills, Canada: Oxford University Press.

Selection in an edited book

> Rogers, A. G. (1998). Understanding changes in girls' relationships and in ego development: Three studies of adolescent girls. In P. M. Westenberg, A. Blasi, & L. D. Cohen (Eds.), *Personality development: Theoretical, empirical, and clinical investigations of Loevinger's conception of ego development* (pp. 145–162). Hillsdale, NJ: Erlbaum.

Article in a journal

> Bell, S. K., & Morgan, S. B. (2000). Children's attitudes and behavioral intentions toward a peer presented as obese: Does a medical explanation for the obesity make a difference? *Journal of Pediatric Psychology, 25*, 137–146.

Note that if there is a volume number the page range is given without "pp." If there is no volume number, include "pp." to indicate that the numbers refer to pagination.

When a journal has continuous pagination, the issue number should not be included. If each issue begins on page 1, give the issue number in parentheses before the page numbers and immediately following the volume number, with no space separating them and a comma following the parentheses. The volume number is italicized; the issue number and its parentheses are not:

> Georgis, D. (2000). Mother nations and the persistence of "not here." *Canadian Woman Studies, 20*(2), 27–34.

Article in a newspaper

> Galloway, G. (2014, March 25). Catholic Church faces human-rights case. *The Globe and Mail*, p. A4.

Note that when a newspaper or magazine article continues on a non-consecutive page, the first page is given, followed by a comma and the page(s) it continues on.

If the newspaper article is unsigned—that is, if it has no listed author—begin the entry with the title:

Pot makes doctors anxious. (2014, March 25). *The Globe and Mail*, p. A10.

Article in a magazine

Walmsley, A. (2001, August). Hoopla! *Report on Business*, 31–34.

Note that if the magazine has both volume and issue numbers, they should be included after the magazine title. For monthly or bi-monthly magazines, give the month(s) in full; for weekly magazines, give the month (in full) and day.

Lecture or presentation

Levenson, A. M. (2008, November). *Withholding treatment in white-coat hypertension*. Paper presented at the meeting of the Canadian Medical Association, Vancouver, Canada.

Electronic sources

Include the same elements as you would for print sources and add any electronic retrieval information which will be helpful in guiding readers to the source. A significant feature of the sixth edition of the *Publication Manual* is the inclusion of new guidelines for referencing electronic sources, with emphasis on the *DOI system* of tracking digital information. Because links can be unstable, a registration agency assigns a *digital object identifier* (DOI) to each article to identify it and provide a means of electronic retrieval. This identifier is a unique alphanumeric string that begins with a 10 and contains a prefix and a suffix separated by a slash (for example, 10.1037/0096-3445). The DOI typically appears near the copyright notice on the first page of the article.

APA style includes the following guidelines for tracking electronic sources:

- Include DOIs in references when they are available; no further retrieval information is required.
- If no DOI is available, write "Retrieved from" and give the URL of the journal's or publisher's homepage. You should provide an exact URL if it will take your reader to the relevant material more reliably.

- If you need to break a URL, do so before most punctuation (but not before "http://") rather than using a hyphen. Don't add a period after the DOI or URL.
- If the source you are using is not included in the following examples, consult the *APA Style Guide to Electronic References* (2012).

Journal article with DOI

Jo, B., Asparouhov, T., Muthen, B. O., Ialongo, N. S., & Brown, C. H. (2008). Cluster randomized trials with treatment noncompliance. *Psychological Methods, 13*(1), 1–18. doi:10.1037/1082-989X.13.1.1

Journal article with no DOI

Hatt, K. (2009). Considering complexity: Toward a strategy for non-linear analysis. *Canadian Journal of Sociology, 34*, 313–348. Retrieved from http://ejournals.library.ualberta.ca/index.php/CJS/index

Online dictionary

Oligarchy. (n.d.). In *Merriam-Webster's online dictionary* (11th ed.). Retrieved from http://www.merriam-webster.com/dictionary/oligarchy

Online encyclopedia

Thagard, P. (2010). Cognitive science. In E. N. Zalta (Ed.), *The Stanford encyclopedia of philosophy* (Summer 2010 ed.). Retrieved from http://plato.stanford.edu/entries/cognitive-science/

Online newspaper article

Jiménez, M. (2009, July 3). Choosing to go gently into that good night. *The Globe and Mail*. Retrieved from http://www.theglobeandmail.com/

Blog post

fuzzbuster. (2014, March 24). New evidence sheds light on the origin of the universe [Web log post]. Retrieved from http://www.thestar .com/news/rethink/2014/03/new_evidence_sheds_light_on_the _origin_of_the_universe.html

Video blog post

> Vegeta, P. (2007, May 4). The killer whales [Video file]. Retrieved from http://www.youtube.com/watch?v=t6H8x0evpTs

Chicago Style

The Chicago Manual of Style (CMS) outlines two methods of documentation.

1. The *notes and bibliography* method, also known as the *humanities style*, is preferred by those in literature, history, and the arts. It uses superscript numerals to direct the reader to footnotes at the bottom of the page or endnotes on a separate page at the end of the document, and it lists all sources in a bibliography at the end of the paper.
2. The *author-date* system, preferred in the physical, natural, and social sciences, follows the same principles as the APA style with only minor stylistic differences.

The Chicago Manual of Style (16th ed., 2010) provides detailed coverage of both methods. Another useful source is the online *Chicago-Style Citation Quick Guide* (www.chicagomanualofstyle.org/tools_citationguide .html).

Notes and bibliography

Below are examples of a note and corresponding bibliographic entry for citations of a variety of materials. In some cases a shortened form of the note is provided; a shortened form should be used when the full bibliographic details of a source have been included in a prior note.

Book with one author

> 1. Michael B. Decter, *Four Strong Winds: Understanding the Growing Challenges to Health Care* (Toronto: Stoddart, 2002), 47.

> 14. Decter, *Four Strong Winds*, 47.

> Decter, Michael B. *Four Strong Winds: Understanding the Growing Challenges to Health Care*. Toronto: Stoddart, 2002.

Book with more than one author

> 1. Ira Marc Price and Linda Comac, *Coping with Macular Degeneration* (New York: Penguin Putnam, 2000), 94–96.

> Price, Ira Marc, and Linda Comac. *Coping with Macular Degeneration*. New York: Penguin Putnam, 2000.

Note that for four or more authors, notes and in-text references give just the first author's name followed by "et al." The bibliography, however, lists all authors' names.

Book with an organization as author

> 1. University of Chicago Press, *The Chicago Manual of Style*, 16th ed. (Chicago: University of Chicago Press, 2010), 656.

> University of Chicago Press. *The Chicago Manual of Style*. 16th ed. Chicago: University of Chicago Press, 2010.

Book with an editor in place of an author

> 1. S. E. Gontarski, ed., *The Grove Press Reader 1951–2001* (New York: Grove, 2001), iv.

> 29. Gontarski, *The Grove Press Reader 1951–2001*, iv.

> Gontarski, S. E., ed. *The Grove Press Reader 1951–2001*. New York: Grove, 2001.

Book with an editor or translator in addition to an author

> 1. Denyse Baillargeon, *Making Do: Women, Family and Home in Montreal during the Great Depression*, trans. Yvonne Klein (Waterloo, ON: Wilfrid Laurier University Press, 1999), 43.

> Baillargeon, Denyse. *Making Do: Women, Family and Home in Montreal during the Great Depression*. Translated by Yvonne Klein. Waterloo, ON: Wilfrid Laurier University Press, 1999.

Chapter or other part of a book

> 1. J. D. Salinger, "Slight Rebellion off Madison," in *Wonderful Town: New York Stories from "The New Yorker,"* ed. David Remnick (New York: Modern Library, 2000), 88.

9. Salinger, "Slight Rebellion off Madison," 88.

Salinger, J. D. "Slight Rebellion off Madison." In *Wonderful Town: New York Stories from "The New Yorker,"* edited by David Remnick, 87–90. New York: Modern Library, 2000.

Article in a journal

1. Taras Kuzio, "Nationalism in Ukraine: Towards a New Framework," *Politics* 20, no. 2 (2000): 77.

22. Kuzio, "Nationalism in Ukraine," 77.

Kuzio, Taras. "Nationalism in Ukraine: Towards a New Framework." *Politics* 20, no. 2 (2000): 77–86.

Article in a journal accessed online

When citing an article in an exclusively online journal or in a print journal that was accessed online, list a Digital Object Identifier (DOI) at the end of the note and bibliographic entry. If a DOI is not available, give the URL.

1. Alan S. Go et al., "Prevalence of Diagnosed Atrial Fibrillation in Adults," *Journal of the American Medical Association* 285, no. 18 (May 9, 2001): 2371, doi:10.1001/jama.285.18.2370.

6. Go et al., "Prevalence of Diagnosed Atrial Fibrillation in Adults," 2371.

Go, Alan S., Elaine M. Hylek, Kathleen A. Phillips, YuChiao Chang, Lori Henault, and Joe Selby. "Prevalence of Diagnosed Atrial Fibrillation in Adults." *Journal of the American Medical Association* 285, no. 18 (May 9, 2001): 2370–75. doi:10.1001/jama.285.18.2370.

Article in a magazine or newspaper

Magazines and newspapers may be cited with a note in the text and need not be included in a bibliography. If a bibliographic entry is required for some particular reason it should appear as follows.

1. Jay Teitel, "Failure to Fail," *Walrus*, April 2008, 44.

Teitel, Jay. "Failure to Fail." *Walrus*, April 2008.

Website or website content

A website should be cited in running text or in a note by means of a title (if applicable—for example, "According to *The Chicago Manual of Style Online* . . ."), the name of the author (if applicable), a descriptive phrase, or a domain name. Websites are often omitted from bibliographies. A note citing original content from a website should include the name of the content author (if applicable), the title or a description of the webpage, a date of publication or modification, and a URL. A bibliographic entry is not typically required, but if one must be provided for some particular reason it should appear as below.

1. "Maritimers to Join Artificial-Hip Lawsuit," *CBC News*, last modified January 13, 2011, http://www.cbc.ca/canada/new-brunswick/story/2011 /01/13/nb-hip-replacement-class-action.html.

CBC. "Maritimers to Join Artificial-Hip Lawsuit." *CBC News*. Last Modified January 13, 2011. http://www.cbc.ca/canada/new-brunswick/story /2011/01/13/nb-hip-replacement-class-action.html.

Blog or blog entry

Blogs should be cited in running text or in a note by means of their title ("In a story reported by *The Huffington Post* . . .") and are often omitted from bibliographies. A note citing a blog entry should include the name of the author, the title of the entry, the title or a description of the blog (the word *blog* should be added in parentheses if it does not already appear in the title), the date of the entry, and the URL. If the blog is a part of a larger publication, list the name of that publication as well. A note citing a comment on a blog entry should include the stated name of the commentator (even if clearly fictitious), the date of the comment, and the words "comment on" followed by the information for the relevant entry. A bibliographic entry is not typically required, but a frequently cited blog may be listed in the bibliography as below.

1. Bob Washick, December 19, 2010 (7:25 p.m.), comment on Tyler Burge, "A Real Science of Mind," *The Stone* (blog), *New York Times*, December 19, 2010, http://opinionator.blogs.nytimes.com/2010/12/19/a-real-science-of-mind/.

Critchley, Simon. *The Stone* (blog). *New York Times*. http://opinionator.blogs .nytimes.com/category/the-stone/.

E-mail message

As with websites and blogs, e-mail messages are usually cited in running text or in a note and are omitted from a bibliography.

> 1. Alex Hemmings, e-mail message to John Smith, May 28, 2014.

Lecture or paper presented at a meeting

> 1. Thomas Hahn, "East and West: Cosmopolitan and Imperial in the Roman Alexander" (paper presented at the annual conference of the Centre for Medieval Studies, Toronto, Canada, March 8–10, 2007).

> Hahn, Thomas. "East and West: Cosmopolitan and Imperial in the Roman Alexander." Paper presented at the annual conference of the Centre for Medieval Studies, Toronto, Canada, March 8–10, 2007.

Author-date

Book with one author

> (Decter 2002, 47)

> Decter, Michael. 2002. *Four Strong Winds: Understanding the Growing Challenges to Health Care*. Toronto: Stoddart.

Book with more than one author

> (Price and Comac 2000, 94–96)

> Price, Ira Marc, and Linda Comac. 2000. *Coping with Macular Degeneration*. New York: Penguin Putnam.

Note that for four or more authors, in-text and parenthetical references give just the first author's name followed by "et al." The reference list, however, lists all authors' names.

Book with an organization as author

> (University of Chicago Press 2010, 656)

> University of Chicago Press. 2010. *The Chicago Manual of Style*. 16th ed. Chicago: University of Chicago Press.

Book with an editor in place of an author

(Gontarski 2001, iv)

Gontarski, S. E., ed. 2001. *The Grove Press Reader 1951–2001*. New York: Grove.

Book with an editor or translator in addition to an author

(Baillargeon 1999, 43)

Baillargeon, Denyse. 1999. *Making Do: Women, Family and Home in Montreal during the Great Depression*. Translated by Yvonne Klein. Waterloo, ON: Wilfrid Laurier University Press.

Chapter or other part of a book

(Salinger 2000, 88)

Salinger, J. D. 2000. "Slight Rebellion off Madison." In *Wonderful Town: New York Stories from "The New Yorker,"* edited by David Remnick, 87–90. New York: Modern Library.

Article in a journal

(Kuzio 2000, 77)

Kuzio, Taras. 2000. "Nationalism in Ukraine: Towards a New Framework." *Politics* 20 (2): 77–86.

Article in a journal accessed online

When citing an article in an exclusively online journal or in a print journal that was accessed online, list a digital object identifier (DOI) at the end of the reference list entry. If a DOI is not available, give the URL.

(Go et al. 2001, 2371)

Go, Alan S., Elaine M. Hylek, Kathleen A. Phillips, YuChiao Chang, Lori Henault, and Joe Selby. 2001. "Prevalence of Diagnosed Atrial Fibrillation in Adults." *Journal of the American Medical Association* 285 (18): 2370–75. doi:10.1001/jama.285.18.2370.

Article in a magazine or newspaper

Magazines and newspapers may be cited with a parenthetical reference in the text and need not be included in a reference list. For instance, the following parenthetical reference would not need to be supplemented by a reference list entry.

(Peter Singer, "The God of Suffering," *Toronto Star*, May 17, 2008)

If a more formal citation is required for some particular reason, the parenthetical reference and reference list entry should appear as below.

(Singer 2008)

Singer, Peter. 2008. "The God of Suffering." *Toronto Star*, May 17.

Website or website content

A website should be cited in running text or in a parenthetical reference by means of a title (if applicable—for example, "According to *The Chicago Manual of Style Online*..."), the name of the author (if applicable), a descriptive phrase, or a domain name. Websites are often omitted from reference lists. When the website's information is included in the reference list, a parenthetical reference should appear in the text.

(CBC 2011)

CBC. 2011. "Maritimers to Join Artificial-Hip Lawsuit." *CBC News*. Last modified January 13. http://www.cbc.ca/canada/new-brunswick /story/2011/01/13/nb-hip-replacement-class-action.html.

Lecture or paper presented at a meeting

(Hahn 2007)

Hahn, Thomas. 2007. "East and West: Cosmopolitan and Imperial in the Roman Alexander." Paper presented at the annual conference of the Centre for Medieval Studies, Toronto, Canada, March 8–10.

CSE Style

The Council of Science Editors (CSE) is the recognized authority on documentation styles in all areas of science and related fields. The following guidelines are based on *Scientific Style and Format: The CSE Manual for Authors, Editors, and Publishers* (8th ed., 2014).

The CSE manual outlines three major systems for documenting sources: name-year, citation-sequence, and citation-name. A brief description of each system follows.

Name-year

This system follows the same principles as the APA system described earlier in this chapter. In-text references consist of the surname of the author and the year of publication enclosed in parentheses. Complete bibliographical information is given in a list of references at the end of the paper organized alphabetically by author surname. In the following examples, note that CSE style emphasizes simplicity, avoiding formatting such as italics and minimizing the use of punctuation:

In-text reference

> Monte Carlo simulations were carried out to compute the escape flux of atomic nitrogen for the low and high solar activity martian thermospheres (Bakalian and Hartle 2006).

End reference

> Bakalian F, Hartle RE. 2006 July. Monte Carlo computations of the escape of atomic nitrogen from Mars. Icarus. 183(1):55–69.

Citation-sequence

In this system, superscript numbers in the text correspond to numbered references in a *References* or *Cited References* section at the end of the document. These references are listed in the order in which they are first cited in the text. Thus, the first reference used in the text will be 1; the next new reference cited will be 2; and so on. Once a source has been assigned a number, it is referred to by that number wherever it appears in the text:

Labossière's groundbreaking study[1] was first challenged by Gormon[2] and later disputed by Huang.[3] In fact, Gormon gained considerable notoriety for her particularly harsh criticism[2] of Labossière's interpretation of the results.[1]

If several sources are being referenced at once, all relevant reference numbers should be given in the same citation. Reference numbers should be separated with commas and no spaces. When using a sequence of three or more citation numbers (e.g., 7, 8, 9), use only the first and last number in the sequence, separated with a hyphen (or an en dash):

Several studies[1,5,12-15] have shown . . .

In the *References* or *Cited References* section, references are listed in order of appearance in the text. For example, if a reference by Wilkins is the first one mentioned in the text, the complete reference to the Wilkins work will be number 1 in the end references.

In-text reference

Self-incompatibility (SI) prevents inbreeding through specific recognition and rejection of incompatible pollen.[1]

End reference

1. Thomas SG, Huang S, Li S, Staiger CJ, Franklin-Tong VE. Actin depolymerization is sufficient to induce programmed cell death in self-incompatible pollen. J Cell Biol. 2006 July 17;174(2):195–207.

Citation-name

In this system, the list of end references is compiled alphabetically by author surname. The references are then numbered in that sequence, with Aaronsen number 1, Babcock number 2, and so on. These numbers are used for in-text references regardless of the sequence in which they appear in the text. If Mortensen is number 38 in the reference list, the in-text reference is number 38, and the same number is used for subsequent in-text references.

When several in-text references occur at the same point, place their corresponding reference list numbers in numeric order. In-text reference numbers not in a continuous sequence are separated by commas with no spaces. For more than two numbers in a continuous sequence, connect the first and last by a hyphen (or an en dash).

> . . . are illustrated in studies[2,7-11,16,25] that corroborate . . .

Formats for end references are similar to those used in the citation-sequence style as shown above.

End references

The following examples illustrate end references for the citation-sequence and citation-name systems of documentation. The name-year system differs by placing the year of publication after the author name(s).

Note that if you cite material you have not read but have seen cited by others you should cite the source of your information about the work; do not cite the original.

Book with one author

> 1. Tomasello M. Constructing a language: a usage-based theory of language acquisition. Cambridge (MA): Harvard University Press; 2003. 388 p.

Note that the last element of the entry ("388 p.") indicates the total number of pages in the book. Although this is an optional component of a book reference, it can provide useful information to the reader.

Book with two or more authors

If the book you are referencing has more than one author, give the names of all authors up to a maximum of 10, after which additional authors are replaced by "et al." Names should be inverted and separated by commas. Note that "and" is not used:

> 2. Peterson LM, Russell AF. Active and passive movement testing. New York (NY): McGraw-Hill; 2002. 418 p.

Book by a group or corporate author

> 3. National Advisory Committee on Immunization. Canadian immunization guide. Ottawa (ON): Canadian Medical Association; 2002. 278 p.

Book with an editor

> 4. Case-Smith J, editor. Pediatric occupational therapy and early intervention. 2nd ed. Boston (MA): Butterworth-Heinemann; 1998. 324 p.

Selection in an edited book

> 5. Rogers AG. Understanding changes in girls' relationships and in ego development: three studies in adolescent girls. In: Westenberg A, Blasi A, Cohen LD, editors. Personality development: theoretical, empirical, and clinical investigations of Loevinger's conception of ego development. Hillsdale (NJ): Erlbaum; 1998. p. 145–162.

Article in a journal

> 6. Baranski JV, Petrusoc WM. Testing architectures of the decision–confidence relation. Can J Exp Psych. 2001;55:196–206.

Note that CSE abbreviates names of journals.

Article in a magazine

> 7. Hollingham R. In the realm of your senses. New Scientist. 2004 Jan 31:40–43.

Article in a newspaper

> 8. MacDonald G. CBC on trial. Globe and Mail. 2001 Jul 28;Sect. R:12 (col. 4).

> 9. Woman again registers her cows as voters. Toronto Star. 2004 Feb 22;Sect. F:2 (col. 6).

Paper presented at meeting

> 10. Reinson G, Drummond K. Past exploration, resources and reserves in the Arctic. Paper presented at: Arctic energy exploration. 2007 Gussow Geoscience Conference; 2007 Oct 15–17; Banff, AB.

Journal article on the Internet

> 11. Pethe V, Bapat B. Molecular genetic etiology of prostate cancer. Open Genomics J. 2008 [accessed 2008 May 29];1:13–21. http://www.bentham.org/open/togenj/openaccess2.htmdoi:10.2174/1874693X00801010013.

Website

12. Preventing skin cancer. Ottawa (ON): Health Canada; 2001 Nov [updated 2004 Feb; accessed 2006 Aug 14]. Available from: http://www.hc-sc.gc.ca/english/iyh/diseases/cancer.html.

Writing an Annotated Bibliography

Some research assignments require an annotated bibliography, which is a standard list of sources accompanied by descriptive or evaluative comments on each item in your list.

If you are asked for an annotated bibliography, begin by arranging your list of entries just as you would for a standard bibliography. Then include a brief comment about the source. You might want to evaluate the quality of the information it contains, the approach of the author, the strengths and/or weaknesses of the source, or its relevance to your subject.

Consult whatever style guide you are using for details about the specific format recommended for an annotated bibliography. The following are examples of typical entries:

MLA

MacMillan, Margaret. *Paris 1919: Six Months that Changed the World*. New York: Random House, 2001. Print. A detailed political history of the events of the peace talks following World War I and their influence on the troubled history of the Balkans, the Middle East, and Iraq.

APA

Kemp, W. H. (2005). *The renewable energy handbook: A guide to rural energy independence, off-grid and sustainable living*. Tamworth, Canada: Aztext Press.

A detailed guide to everything an off-grid home should have, with comprehensive treatment of photovoltaic electricity generation, wind energy, micro hydro electricity production, batteries, and inverters.

Chicago (notes and bibliography)

Marcus, Greil. *Mystery Train: Images of America in Rock 'n' Roll Music.* 4th ed. New York: Plume, 1997.

A literary approach to popular music, including a classic chapter on Elvis and an insightful analysis of the music of The Band. Provides cultural criticism and concrete evidence of unities in the American imagination.

Chicago (author-date)

Dallaire, Roméo. 2003. *Shake Hands with the Devil.* Toronto: Random House.

A first-hand account of the 1994 genocide by the force commander of the UN Assistance Mission for Rwanda, this book recounts the events leading up to the deaths of 800,000 Rwandans in what is often described as the greatest failure of the United Nations.

Giving an Oral Presentation

8

> **In this chapter, we will examine**
> - strategies for preparing and delivering an effective oral presentation;
> - tips for producing and using visual aids; and
> - guidelines for giving a group presentation.

Introduction

For some students the prospect of standing in front of a class to give a seminar can be terrifying. The reason some students dread having to speak to a group is almost always that they are afraid of appearing foolish by not knowing what to say or how to answer questions. But there is no reason you can't give a good presentation even if you're nervous when you begin—you just have to be prepared.

If you think about all the bad seminars you've heard in class, you will readily remember some problems they shared: you couldn't follow the speaker's reasoning or understand some points; the talk was too detailed; or the speaker simply droned on in a manner that bored you. On the other hand, the good seminars you have listened to were likely well organized and led you through the material in a systematic and clear way. They held your attention.

Some individuals are naturally more comfortable in front of an audience than others, and these students do have a slight advantage. However, you will find that even if public speaking is not one of your natural talents, you can still achieve results by following a few simple rules. Underlying the whole process is the most important rule of all: *Connect with your audience.*

Preparing Your Talk

Know your topic

For the purposes of an in-class seminar, you are the expert and will probably know more about your topic than any of the other students will. You need to show your audience that your grasp of the subject matter goes beyond what you include in your talk. If you know no more than what you present, you will not be able to answer questions. The more background reading you do, the more information you will have to fall back on when someone asks you a question. This can be a confidence booster.

Consider your audience

It is a mistake to prepare a seminar based on what you know about your topic. In fact, you should approach the talk from precisely the opposite direction: put yourself in the position of your audience. If you were sitting in class instead of standing up at the front, what would you expect of the speaker? How much will the typical audience member know about this topic? What will the typical audience member find most interesting? Most relevant? What can you take for granted as common knowledge in the context of the course? If you combine these with your own question—What do I want my audience to know?—then you have the basis for setting up a talk that will connect with your audience.

Create an outline

Decide on the key points you want to make. Since an audience cannot possibly digest all that you know, simplify the material. Many polished speakers keep these key points to three and then add backup details and examples to drive those points home. In creating an outline, use point form wherever you can. These short messages become the heart of your talk.

Plan to talk rather than read

Many beginning speakers feel they must write everything down. Sometimes writing helps to shape and simplify their material. However, a presentation is not an essay, and it is a mistake to simply read a talk. Your reading voice, unless you are a trained actor, will be too fast and too flat to engage your audience.

Memorizing your entire talk will likely have the same monotonous effect as reading. Besides, you will be nervous about forgetting some parts. Instead, use your point-form outline as your only guide, putting it on index cards you can hold in your hand easily. If you are worried that you may freeze when you first begin, write out the first one or two sentences of what you want to say, just to get started.

Rehearse

Practise speaking with just your note outline. You will be forced to use your own words to fill in the points, creating a natural speaking style. Think of your presentation as a conversation with your audience. If you can, have a friend pretend to be your audience. Rehearsing is a much better solution for nerves than is reading or memorizing. Each time you rehearse, your talk will become smoother and you will be more confident. Equally important, rehearsing will let you know in advance if you have too little material, or, as is most often the case, too much. A common speaking error is to talk beyond the allotted time. Knowing that you will annoy the audience if you speak too long, or even be cut off, can create a rushed, ungraceful finish.

No matter how familiar you are with your technology, if you are using it to present visual aids, check out the process in your rehearsal and then check it again just before you deliver your talk. Countless presentations have been delayed or damaged when the technology does not work immediately.

Consider preparing a handout

Providing an outline of your talk to your audience may help them remember points or understand your organization. Be sure it is brief, not a repeat of your whole talk, if you want people to pay attention to the presentation. When you do need to give out detailed information, leave it until after your presentation, since the handout will likely be read from start to finish before you are halfway through talking, sapping interest in what you are saying.

Preparing Visual Aids

With the advanced technology available today, your ability to use visual aids is limited only by your own ingenuity and the instructor's willingness to let you use the technology in class. Videos and slide shows can add life to a talk. They can reinforce the main points for the audience and can also serve as a reminder for you. At times they can be a comfort because they draw attention away from you and onto the screen.

They can also be overused, a too-handy crutch that deflects energy from the speech itself. Consider them as ancillary to the main event—to what you are saying. Use them to enhance your talk, not deliver it for you.

The suggestions that follow apply to any visuals that you might want to display during a talk.

Keep it simple

The saying "Less is more" is a good one to remember. It is much better to put too little material on a slide than too much. Three or 4 lines of print are the ideal, not 10 or 12.

- **Use plain fonts.** Unless you need a fancy one for a specific reason, stick with fonts that are easy to read. Fonts that are too elaborate reduce readability. Another caution: if the computer in the classroom does not have the same font you used on your home computer, it will substitute a different one. This will play havoc with your formatting, changing the spacing and design of your slides. It's prudent to stick with something traditional.
- **Choose an appropriate font size.** The last thing you want on your visuals is text that is too small to decipher. The regular 12-point font you use for your papers will almost certainly be too small when it is projected on a screen. One rule of thumb suggests 36 points for titles and 24 for body text.
- **Use a simple background.** If you're using PowerPoint to make your slides, choose a plain background and use the same one on every slide.
- **Don't overuse colour or animation.** Unless you have a good reason for doing so, avoid multicoloured slides or animation effects that are too busy or distracting.
- **Don't put too much information on one slide.** If you treat your slides as a script, then you'll be tempted to read directly from them. Instead, make your point briefly on the slide and then expand on the material as you talk. This will make your presentation sound much more natural and professional. If you have a diagram or graph, use the simplest version that you can.
- **Don't use too many slides.** A common weakness in presentations is overuse of slides, suggesting that the speaker cannot manage to talk without a prop. Try at the beginning of your presentation to establish a rapport with the audience by talking briefly without a slide. Then, after you finish your last slide, try to put the focus back on you as a person talking to other people, even if you speak as a representative of an organization.

- **Have a trial run.** You have likely witnessed presentations where technical difficulties caused embarrassment for both the speaker and the audience. Be sure to test drive your presentation in the room where you'll be presenting your talk so that you can troubleshoot before you have an audience.

Keep it organized

The second fundamental rule of using visual aids is to make sure your material is well organized. If you use a consistent organizational scheme, the audience will become used to it and will be able to follow along more easily.

- **Begin with a title slide.** A title slide sets the tone and orients the audience to your topic. It should contain the title, your name, and the name of the course.
- **Create a summary slide.** This will give an outline of your talk so that your audience knows what to expect.
- **Use headings and subheadings.** Most of your slides should be in point form, using numbers or bullets, with headings and subheadings. If you do this, the audience will be able to tell which are your main points and which are elaborations.
- **Consider section breaks.** If your talk falls naturally into several sections, you could start each one with a new title slide. Anything that allows the audience to see the structure of your talk is worth doing.

Delivering Your Talk

Dress comfortably

Dressing comfortably means not overdressing but also not dressing down for the occasion. For a presentation that simulates the business world, your instructor may expect you to wear a suit. A suit also suggests the importance of a talk. However, for most student presentations, if you ordinarily wear jeans and a short-sleeved shirt to class, it may look odd to give your presentation in a suit. When in doubt, find out what is expected. Just don't go too far with informal dress: ripped jeans and an old T-shirt can seem disrespectful to the audience. Something that's casual but clean and neat will set a better tone.

Give yourself time at the beginning

If you have equipment to set up or other preparations to make, be sure to do this before the class begins if you can. If everything is ready, you won't get flustered trying to resolve technical problems with your classmates looking on.

Begin with an overview

If the audience knows how the talk is structured, they will be able to understand what you are doing as you move from one point to another. Introduce your topic and then give a brief statement of the main areas you will discuss. Again, a summary slide or handout with the topic outline is useful because the audience can refer to it as your talk progresses.

Project your voice

When you speak, be sure you're loud enough so that everyone in the classroom can hear you. Also, try to put some feeling into what you say. It is difficult to remain attentive to even the most interesting presentation delivered in a monotone.

Don't be apologetic

The worst way to start a talk is by saying: "You'll have to forgive me, I'm really nervous about this," or "I hope this projector is going to work properly." Even if you are nervous, try to create an air of confidence.

Maintain eye contact with your audience

Look around the room as you speak. When you look at individuals, you involve them in what you are saying. Also, as you scan the faces in front of you, you can monitor for signs of boredom or incomprehension and can adjust your talk accordingly.

Use visual aids effectively

If you have visual aids, take advantage of them; just remember that the visual material should only enhance your talk, not deliver it for you. Some of the following guidelines may help you when you are using visual aids:

- When you are making a point from your slide, try to use different words and expand on what is there.
- Give your audience enough time to read through each visual. They will find it frustrating to see images, overheads, or slides flash by before they've had a chance to take them in.

- Explain your figures. If it's a graph, describe what the x- and y-axes represent, and then explain what the graph shows. If it's a diagram, take the audience through it step by step; you may be familiar with the material, but your audience might not be.
- Take care not to block the audience's view of the material on the screen. Stand a bit to the side.
- When referring to something on the screen, you can use a wooden or laser pointer. That said, always turn to face the audience *before* speaking. Talking to the screen disconnects you from listeners.

Don't go too fast

A good talk is one that is well paced. If you're discussing background information that everyone is familiar with, you can go over it a little faster; if you're describing something complex or less familiar, go slowly. It often helps to explain a complicated point a couple of times in slightly different ways. Don't be afraid to ask your audience if they understand. Almost certainly, someone will speak up if there is a problem.

Monitor your time allotment

As well as pacing your delivery, you should try to ensure that you aren't going to finish too quickly, or worse, go over your allotted time. If you've rehearsed your talk, you should know roughly how long it will take. Remember to allow extra time for questions that people might ask during your talk. Ideally, you should plan to make your talk a little shorter than the amount of time you have available so that you have some leeway to answer questions.

End on a strong note

Don't let your talk fade away at the end. You should finish by summarizing the main points you have made and drawing some conclusions. These conclusions should be available on your visual material so that they can be left there for the discussion. If you can raise some questions in your conclusions, this will set you up for the question period to follow.

Be prepared for questions

The question period is a time when you can really make a good impression. This is an opportunity for you to demonstrate your thorough understanding of the topic and even to reinforce one or two points that you think you may have missed. If you know your material well, you should have no problem dealing with the content of the questions, but the manner in which you answer these questions is important too:

- It's a good idea to repeat a question if you are in a large room where everyone may not have heard it. This act should also solidify the question in your mind and give you a few extra moments to consider it before answering.
- If you didn't hear or didn't understand a question, don't be afraid to ask the person who asked it to repeat or clarify it.
- Keep your answers short and to the point. Rambling answers are not helpful to anyone. If you don't know an answer, say so. It's okay to admit that you don't know everything—as long as you don't do this for every question. And, certainly, it's better to admit that you don't know an answer than to guess or to make up a response that everyone will know is not correct.

Group Presentations

Group presentations are common in many different areas of study. Collaboration helps share the load and often makes it easier to overcome the fear of public speaking. In Chapter 5, we discussed how to be effective in preparing a group business report. Those guidelines also hold true for group presentations on other topics.

Delivering a group presentation for a class assignment usually requires each member to have approximately the same speaking time. Managing only the technology, if you are using visuals, is usually not sufficient participation, so be sure to check with your instructor about the course requirements.

You may find it helpful to have one member introduce the topic and speakers and then give a brief summary or conclusion at the end. This approach will provide a sense of organization and cohesion in the presentation. If the strongest speaker is given this task, it can also add force to the presentation. On the other hand, a relatively weak or fearful speaker will be noticed less if positioned in the middle.

Occasionally in a group presentation the team has to grapple with a difficult member who won't cooperate or doesn't contribute. If the team is not voluntary but is selected by the instructor, this can be a tricky situation. Much depends on previous relations with the difficult member, what the others in the group think, the preparation time constraints, and the importance of the particular exercise. Taking all into account, the decision will likely be either to try for some compromise or to force agreement or participation through majority rule. Of course, if the difficult member can simply leave and join another group, the problem is more easily solved.

Rehearse together and rehearse as many times as possible. Nothing will improve your results as much as running through the whole presentation as a group. You will be able to adjust the timing if need be. As you observe and listen to the others, you may be able to make suggestions that will help individuals or the group as a whole. Phrase your suggestions in a positive way. Often a group presentation is as much an exercise in cooperation as in speaking. Remember that it's a team effort, with the same challenges and rewards as any team sport.

Writing Examinations

> **In this chapter, we will examine**
> - helpful steps in preparing for exams and tests;
> - strategies for writing essay exams, including open-book and take-home exams; and
> - tips for writing objective tests.

Introduction

Most students feel nervous before tests and exams. It's not surprising. Writing an essay exam imposes special pressures. You can't write and rewrite the way you can in a regular essay, you must often write on topics you would otherwise choose to avoid, and you must observe strict time limits. On the surface, objective tests, such as multiple-choice tests, may seem easier because you don't have to compose the answers, but they force you to be more decisive about your answers than essay exams do and they require highly detailed and precise knowledge of the subject. To do your best you need to feel calm—but how? These general guidelines will help you approach any test or exam with confidence.

Preparing for the Exam

Review regularly

Exam preparation has to begin long before the exam period itself. A weekly review of lecture notes and texts will help you remember important material and relate new information to old. If you don't review regularly, at the end of the year you'll be faced with relearning rather than remembering.

Set memory triggers

As you review, condense and focus the material by writing down in the margin key words or phrases that will trigger whole sets of details in your mind. The trigger might be a concept word that names or points to an important theory or definition, or it might be a quantitative phrase such as "three causes of the decline of manufacturing" or "five reasons for inflation."

Sometimes you can create an acronym or a nonsense sentence that will trigger an otherwise hard-to-remember set of facts—something like the acronym HOMES (Huron, Ontario, Michigan, Erie, Superior) for the Great Lakes. Since the difficulty of memorizing increases with the number of individual items you are trying to remember, any method that reduces the number of items to be memorized will increase your effectiveness.

Ask questions: Try the three-C approach

Think of questions that will get to the heart of the material and force you to examine the relations between various subjects or issues; then think about how you would answer them. The three-C approach discussed on pages 11–13 may help. For example, reviewing the *components* of the subject could mean focusing on the main parts of an issue or on the definitions of major terms or theories. When reviewing *change* in the subject, you might ask yourself what the causes or results of those changes are. To review *context* you might consider how certain aspects of the subject—issues, theories, actions, results—compare with others in the course. Essentially, the three-C approach forces you to look at the material from different perspectives.

Copies of exams from previous years are useful both for learning the types of questions you might be asked and for checking on the thoroughness of your preparation. If old exams aren't available, you might get together with classmates and ask each other questions. Just remember that the most useful review questions are not the ones that require you to recall facts but the ones that force you to analyze, integrate, or evaluate information.

Identify special needs

Educational institutions are now making a concerted effort to recognize and accommodate the special needs of students who have learning disabilities such as dyslexia or other perceptual problems or physical disabilities. If you think you fall into this category, be sure to make your instructor and the appropriate school officials aware of your situation. You may be able to complete a test in a computer lab or under special conditions that will give you the best chance to demonstrate your knowledge.

Allow extra time

Give yourself lots of time to get to the exam. Nothing is more nerve-wracking than thinking you're going to be late because your alarm didn't go off or you got caught in traffic. Remember Murphy's Law: "Whatever can go wrong will." Anticipate any potential difficulties and allow yourself a good margin.

Writing an Essay Exam

Read the exam

An exam is not a 100-metre dash. Instead of starting to write immediately, take time at the beginning to read through each question and create a plan. A few minutes spent on thinking and organizing will bring better results than the same time spent on writing a few more lines.

Apportion your time

Read the instructions carefully to find out how many questions you must answer and to see if you have any choice. Subtract five minutes or so for the initial planning, and then divide the time you have left by the number of questions you have to answer. If possible, allow for a little extra time at the end to reread and edit your work. If the instructions on the exam indicate that not all questions are of equal value, apportion your time accordingly.

Choose your questions

Decide on the questions that you will do and the order in which you will do them. Your answers don't have to be in the same order as the questions. If you think you have lots of time, it's a good idea to place your best answer first, your worst answer in the middle, and your second-best answer at the end, in order to leave the reader on a high note. If you think you will be rushed, though, it's wiser to work from best to worst; that way you will be sure to get all the marks you can on your good answers, and you won't have to cut a good answer short at the end.

Stay calm

If your first reaction on reading the exam is "I can't do any of this!" force yourself to be calm; take several slow, deep breaths to relax; then decide which question you can answer best. Even if the exam seems impossible at first, you can probably find one question that looks manageable; that's the one to begin with. It will get you rolling and increase your confidence. By the time you have finished your first answer, you will probably find that your mind has worked through to the answer for another question.

Read each question carefully

As you turn to each question, read it again carefully and underline all the key words. The wording will probably suggest the number of parts your answer should have. Be sure you don't overlook anything—this is a common mistake when people are nervous. Since the verb used in the question is usually a guide for the approach to take in your answer, it's especially important that you interpret the key words in the question correctly. In Chapter 2 we summarized what you should do when you are faced with instructions like *explain, compare, discuss*, and so on; it's a good idea to review this list before you go to the exam (see page 13).

Make notes

Before you even begin to organize your answer, jot down key ideas and information related to the topic on rough paper or the unlined pages of your answer book. These notes will save you the worry of forgetting something while you are writing. Next, arrange those parts you want to use into a brief plan.

Be direct

Get to the points quickly and use examples to illustrate them. In an exam, as opposed to an essay, it's best to use a direct approach. Don't worry about composing a graceful introduction; simply state the main points that you are going to discuss and then get on with developing them. Remember that your paper will likely be one of many read and marked by someone who has to work quickly; the clearer your answers are, the better they will be received. For each main point give the kind of specific details that will prove you really know the material. General statements will show you are able to assimilate information, but they need examples to back them up.

Write legibly

Poor handwriting makes readers cranky. When the person marking your paper has to struggle to decipher your ideas, you may get poorer marks than you deserve. If for some special reason (such as a physical disability) your writing is hard to read, you should be able to make special arrangements to use a computer. If your writing is not very legible, consider printing. Also, write on every second or third line of the booklet; this will not only make your writing easier to read but also leave you space to make changes and additions if you have time later on.

Stick to your time plan

Stay on schedule and don't skip any questions. Try to write something on each topic. Remember that it's easier to score half marks for a question you don't know much about than it is to score full marks for one you could write pages on. If you find yourself running out of time on an answer and still haven't finished, summarize the remaining points and go on to the next question. Leave a large space between questions so that you can go back and add more if you have time.

Reread your answers

No matter how tired or fed up you are, reread your answers at the end if there's time. Check especially for clarity of expression; try to get rid of confusing sentences and improve your transitions so that the logical connections between your ideas are as clear as possible. Revisions that make answers easier to read are always worth the effort.

Writing an Open-Book Exam

If you think that permission to take your books into the exam room is an "open sesame" to success, be forewarned: do not fall into the trap of relying too heavily on your reference materials. You may spend so much time riffling through pages and looking things up that you won't have time to write good answers. The result may be worse than if you had been allowed no books at all.

If you want to do well, use your books only to check information and look up specific, hard-to-remember details for a topic you already know a good deal about. For instance, if your subject is history, you can look up exact dates or quotations; for an economics test, you can look up statistics; for an exam in social theory, you can check some classical references and find the authors' exact definitions of key concepts—if you know where to find them quickly. In other words, use the books to make sure your answers are precise and well illustrated, but never use them to replace studying and careful exam preparation.

Writing a Take-Home Exam

The benefit of a take-home exam is that you have time to plan your answers and consult your texts and other sources. However, usually there is still a time limit. Don't work yourself into a frenzy trying to respond with a polished research essay for each question; instead, aim for well-written exam answers. Keep in mind that you were given this assignment to test your overall command of the course material; your reader is likely to be less concerned with your specialized research than with evidence that you have understood and assimilated the material.

The guidelines for a take-home exam are similar to those for a regular exam; the only difference is that you don't need to keep such a close eye on the clock:

- Keep your introductions short and get to the point quickly.
- Organize your answers in such a way that they are straightforward and clear and the reader can easily see your main ideas.
- Use concrete examples to back up your points.
- Where possible, show the range of your knowledge of course material by referring to a variety of sources rather than constantly using the same ones.
- Try to show that you can analyze and evaluate material—that you can do more than simply repeat information.
- If you are asked to acknowledge the sources of any quotations you use, be sure to jot them down as you go rather than trying to track down sources at the end.

Writing an Objective Test

Objective tests are particularly common in the social sciences, but they are used by instructors in other disciplines as well. Although they sometimes contain true-false questions, they usually feature multiple-choice questions. The main difficulty is that the questions are designed to confuse the student who is not certain of the correct answers. If you tend to second-guess yourself or if you are the sort of person who readily sees two sides to every question, you may find objective tests particularly hard at first. Fortunately, practice almost always improves performance.

Preparation for objective tests is the same as for other exams. Here, though, it's especially important to pay attention to definitions and unexpected or confusing pieces of information, because these are the kinds of details that are often used in questions for objective tests. Although there is no sure recipe for doing well on an objective test—other than a thorough knowledge of the course material—the following suggestions may help you do better.

Find out the marking system

If marks are based solely on the number of right answers, you should pick an answer for every question even if you aren't sure it's the right one. For a true-false question you have a 50 per cent chance of being right. Even for a multiple-choice question with four possible answers, you have a 25 per cent chance of getting it right, more if you can eliminate one or more of the wrong answers.

On the other hand, if there is a penalty for wrong answers—if marks are deducted for errors—you should guess only when you're fairly sure you're right, or when you're able to rule out most of the possibilities. Don't make wild guesses.

Do the easy questions first

Go through the test at least twice. On the first round, don't waste time on troublesome questions. Since the questions are usually of equal value, it's best to get all the marks you can on the ones you find easy. You can tackle the more difficult questions on the next round. This approach has two advantages: first, you won't be forced, because you have run out of time, to leave out any questions that you could easily have answered correctly; second, when you come back to a difficult question on the second round, you may find that in the meantime you have figured out the answer.

Make your guesses educated ones

If you have to guess, at least increase your chances of getting the answer right. Forget about intuition, hunches, and lucky numbers. More importantly, forget about so-called patterns of correct answers—the idea that if there have been two "A" answers in a row, the next one can't possibly be "A" as well, or that if there hasn't been a "true" for a while, "true" must be a good guess. Many test setters either don't worry about patterns at all or else deliberately elude pattern hunters by giving the right answer the same letter or number several times in a row.

Remember that constructing good objective tests is a special skill that not all instructors have mastered. In many cases the questions they pose, though sound enough as questions, do not produce enough realistic alternatives for answers. In such cases the test setter may resort to some less realistic options, and if you keep your eyes open you can spot them. James F. Shepherd has suggested a number of tips that will increase your chances of making the right guess:

- Start by weeding out all the answers you know are wrong rather than looking for the right one.
- Avoid any terms you don't recognize. Some students are taken in by anything that looks like sophisticated terminology and may assume that such answers must be correct. In fact, these answers are usually wrong; the unfamiliar term may well be a red herring, especially if it's close in sound to the correct one.
- Avoid extremes. Most often the right answer lies in between. For example, suppose that the options are the numbers 800,000; 350,000; 275,000; and 15: the highest and lowest numbers are likely to be wrong.
- Avoid absolutes, especially on questions dealing with people. Few aspects of human life are as certain as is implied by such words as *everyone, all, no one, always, invariably,* or *never.* Statements containing these words are usually false.
- Avoid jokes or humorous statements.
- Avoid demeaning or insulting statements. Like jokes, these are usually inserted simply to provide a full complement of options.
- Choose the particular statement over the general (generalizations are usually too sweeping to be true).
- Choose "all of the above" over individual answers. Test setters know that students with a patchy knowledge of the course material will often fasten on the one fact they know. Only those with a thorough knowledge will recognize that all the answers listed are correct.[1]

If you have time at the end of the exam, go back and reread the questions. One or two wrong answers caused by misreading can make a significant difference to your score. On the other hand, don't start second-guessing yourself and changing a lot of answers at the last minute. Studies have shown that when students make changes they are often wrong. Stick with your original decisions unless you know for certain that you have made a mistake.

Note

1. Adapted from James F. Shepherd, *College Study Skills*, 6th ed. (Boston: Houghton Mifflin, 2002) and *RSVP: The College Reading, Study, and Vocabulary Program*, 5th ed. (Boston: Houghton Mifflin, 1996).

Writing a Resumé and Letter of Application

10

In this chapter, we will examine

- tips for writing a resumé in either standard or functional format;
- suggestions for writing an effective letter of application; and
- guidelines for electronic applications for graduate school or employment.

Introduction

Whether you are looking for a summer job, applying to graduate school, or seeking permanent employment, eventually you will have to write a resumé and letter of application. You may even need to write an application letter for some courses or programs, including those with work placement. The person who reads your application will not have time to read reams of material, so you will need to be brief yet precise.

Although paper applications are sometimes preferred in conservative institutions or for some high-level positions, electronic applications are now the norm. This chapter will give you guidelines that apply to both methods of delivery. Consider both to have similar content and formatting—and a similar need for careful preparation.

Writing a Resumé

Choosing the best content

Think of a resumé as more than just a summary of facts; think of it as a marketing strategy tailored to specific employers. You will need to supply some basic information, but how you organize it and which details you emphasize are up to you. One good strategy is to put your most important or relevant qualifications first, so that they are noticed at first glance. For most students this means leading with educational qualifications, but for others it may mean starting with work experience. Within each section of your resumé use reverse chronological order so that the most recent item is at the beginning.

Whatever arrangement you choose, your goal is to keep the resumé as concise as possible while including all the specific information that will help you "sell" yourself. A reader will lose interest in a resumé that goes on and on, mixing trivial details with the pertinent ones. On the other hand, experience or skills that may seem irrelevant to you may, in fact, demonstrate an important attribute or qualification, such as a sense of responsibility or willingness to work hard. For example, working as a part-time short-order cook may be significant if you state that this was how you paid your way through university.

The tone of a resumé should be upbeat, so don't draw attention to any potential weaknesses you may have, such as lack of experience in a particular area. Never list a category and then write "None"—you don't want to suggest that you lack something. Remember to adjust your list of special skills to fit each job you apply for so that the reader will see at a glance that you meet the job requirements. Finally, never claim more for yourself than is true; lying on a resumé can be grounds for firing, or even legal action, if it is discovered later.

You are not required to state anything about your age, place of birth, marital status, race, religion, sex, or sexual orientation. One possible exception is affirmative action (AA) or equal employment opportunity (EEO) employers who ask potential candidates to indicate if they are members of a minority or under-represented group. As a general rule, if you are completing an application form with set questions it is a good idea to provide all the information requested; if you don't, your application may be ignored.

Here is a list of common resumé information, along with some suggestions on how to present it. The examples on pages 132–4 show the two different ways of presenting this information depending on the kind of background and experience you have.

- **Name.** Your name is typically placed in capital letters and centred at the top of the page, although there are many options, including a number of templates available through your word-processing program.
- **Contact information.** This can include your mailing address with postal code, home phone and cellphone numbers, e-mail address, and website address if you have one. If you have a temporary student address, remember to indicate where you can be reached at other times.

- **Career objective (optional).** It's often helpful to let the employer know your career goal, or at least your current aim for employment, for example, "a junior planning position with opportunity for advancement."
- **Education.** Include any degrees, diplomas, or certificates, along with the institution that granted them and the dates. If it will help your case and if you are short of other qualifications, you may also list courses you have taken that are relevant to the job. In a functional resumé, educational background may be included under a heading such as *Skills* or *Abilities* (see page 135).
- **Awards or honours.** These may be in a separate section or included with your education details.
- **Work experience.** Give the name and location of your employer, along with your job title and the dates of employment. Instead of outlining your duties (which an employee may or may not carry out well), list your accomplishments on the job, using point form and action verbs. For example:
  - Designed and administered a public-awareness survey.
  - Supervised a three-member field crew.
  In a functional resumé, work experience is often included under headings like *Marketing Background* or *Business Experience*.
- **Research experience or specialized skills.** This is a chance to list information that may give you an advantage in a competitive market, such as experience with certain computer programs or knowledge of a second language. If you have worked as a research assistant, be sure to state the type of work you did and the name of your employer, for example:

  > Assisted Professor Marika Szabo in a laboratory research project on "The Liquid Limit of Leda Clay," Carleton University, Summer 2014.

- **Other interests** (optional). Depending on the employer and the amount of information you have already included, you may choose to omit this section. Sometimes, however, including a few achievements or interests, such as travel or athletic or musical accomplishments, will show that you are well rounded or especially disciplined, and if the employer shares some of your interests they can be a valuable trigger during an interview. However, avoid a long list of items that merely show passive or minimal involvement.
- **References** (optional). The value of references is changing. In the past, written letters of reference were a useful part of many applications. However, increased worry about lawsuits means that many referees are reluctant to give any negative comments. Thus employers are less likely

to rely on such letters, especially if they are attached to an application. A letter written in confidence and sent directly to the potential employer at his or her request carries more weight.

As result, an acceptable approach is to say on the application that "references are available on request." If you currently have a job and hope to move to a new one, your work experience matters. However, a potential employer normally knows better than to contact your current employer without your explicit permission, and this will only happen when the applicant has become a top candidate. Even then, a telephone conversation or two is usually more reliable than a written reference, since explicit questions or concerns can be addressed directly.

However, if you are a student or recent graduate without a record of employment in your chosen field, a reference letter can still be useful. From someone who knows you well and has credibility, it can underline important character traits: diligence, skill with people, creativity, or reliability, to name just a few. A sports coach, a professor who has worked with you closely, or the manager of a part-time job you had in any field are all suitable choices. Avoid using relatives or close family friends, who could have a conflict of interest. Depending on how respected or well-known the referee, a letter can help set you above the pack of applicants, but don't count on it.

Whether you choose to list potential referees up front or wait until after an interview, be sure to contact them for permission ahead of time to ensure that they are willing to act in this capacity. Obtain their preferred contact information, including complete mailing and email address and phone number. If, as is likely, you have not presented it on the application beforehand, have your list neatly typed and ready to hand to an interviewer. This preparation will avoid delays which could drop you down the list, giving other candidates an advantage.

Preparing a standard resumé

If you're a recent graduate without a great deal of work experience, the standard resumé format will probably show your qualifications in their best light. It includes separate headings for education and work experience and uses a reverse chronological order within those sections. At first, you may need to include all summer and part-time jobs, even if they aren't particularly related to your field. As you gain more experience, you can begin dropping some of the less relevant positions and focusing on those that are significant for the kind of job you're seeking.

RAJ CHOUDHURY

Present Address (until 1 April 2014):	Permanent Address:
123 College Rd	45 Main St
Toronto ON M3J 1P3	Ottawa ON K1S 5B6
Phone: 416-123-4567	Phone: 613-456-0000
Fax: 416-123-4568	Fax: 613-456-0001
rchdhry@yorku.ca	choudhury@cogeco.ca

Career Objective: an entry-level position in the pulp and paper industry, in field research or administration, where my background in environmental studies and geography would be an asset

Education:

- M.Sc. in Environmental Studies, York University, expected in May 2014 (Thesis: "The Links between Government Policy and Forest Clearance in BC")
- B.A. (Honours Geography) Carleton University, 2012

Honours and Awards:

- Dean's List, 2010–2012, Carleton University
- Cailey Award for highest marks in Geography, Carleton University

Work Experience:

Summer 2013 – Research Assistant for Professor Gary Smithers in field study of "Perceptions of Place in a Rural-Urban Fringe Environment" in Mexico

- helped develop questionnaire and conduct interviews
- prepared analysis of findings

Summer 2012 – Head of tree-planting crew for Planters Inc. in northern Ontario

- hired, trained, and supervised crew of eight planters
- organized delivery of equipment and food supplies
- managed budget and kept accounts

Summers 2010–2012 – Member of tree-planting crew for Planters Inc

- earned enough to pay my way through university

Specialized Skills and Experience:

- extensive knowledge of Microsoft Office, Target, Safeguard, AutoCAD, Photoshop, and Illustrator

- strong background in field research, including several advanced courses in field research and the opportunity to use these skills in my position as Research Assistant
- skilled in air photo interpretation and comphuter-assisted cartography

Interests and Achievements:

- Captain of Carleton University hockey team, 2010–2012
- Big Brother (Toronto chapter) since August 2009

References: available upon request

Preparing a functional resumé

If your background is less conventional, with a wide range of experience or a change in direction, a functional resumé may be the best format, as it gives greater flexibility to stress transferable skills. Most functional resumés include categories for different areas of expertise (for example, *Research*, *Administration*, *Sales*). Others may focus on personal attributes such as initiative, teamwork, analytic ability, or communication skills.

REBECCA McLEAN
16 Harbour St
Halifax NS B3H 2L4
902-491-3020
rmclean@sympatico.ca

Career Objective: work in promotions or fundraising in a public-sector organization

Profile: an energetic, bilingual communicator with a record of initiative

Communication Skills:

- Honours B.A. in English, Dalhousie University, June 2014; 3.70 GPA
- Sports & Entertainment Editor for Dalhousie student newspaper, 2012–14; reporter, 2010–12
- debated regularly as a member of Dalhousie's Debating Society
- volunteer tour guide for University, Summer 2011
- fluent in French, both written and spoken

Initiative:

- Founded my own dried-flower business, Flower Fancies, when still in school (2009–10). Designed and sold arrangements and kept accounts, earning enough to pay for my first year at Dalhousie.
- Organized, with two other students, an environmental awareness week at Dalhousie University (2012). Responsible for enlisting and managing 40 volunteers.

Other Achievements and Activities:

- member of Dalhousie tennis team (2012–14)
- play guitar and sing in blues band

References:

Professor James Stark	Mrs. Margarita Navarro
Department of English	Student Affairs Director
Dalhousie University	Dalhousie University
Halifax NS B3H 3J5	Halifax NS B3H 3J5
902-491-0000	902-491-0001
jstark@dalhousie.ca	mnavarro@dalhousie.ca

Writing a Letter of Application

You should not use the same letter for all applications; instead, you should craft each one to focus directly on the particular job and company in question and catch the attention of each particular reader. In a sense, both the resumé and the letter of application are intended to open the door to the next stage in the job hunt: the interview. The key is to link your skills to the position, not just to state information. What matters is not what you want but what the employer needs.

One challenge in writing a letter of application is to tell your reader about yourself and your qualifications without seeming egotistical. Two tips can help:

1. Limit the number of sentences beginning with *I*. Instead, try burying *I* in the middle of some sentences, where it will be less noticeable, for example, "For two months last summer, I worked as a . . ."
2. Avoid, as much as possible, making unsupported, subjective claims. Instead of saying "I am a highly skilled manager," say something

like, "Last summer, I managed a $250,000 field study with a crew of seven assistants." Rather than "I have excellent research skills," you might say, "Based on my previous work, Professor Kimiko Sunahara selected me from twenty applicants to help with her summer research work."

Here is an example (not to be copied rigidly) of an application letter that tries to connect the applicant's background with the needs of the company:

---

205 Franklin Drive
Ottawa ON K1N 8W5
1 April 2014

Steven Nazar
Personnel Director
Outlands Developments
110 Duplessis Blvd.
Ottawa ON K1S 5B6

Dear Mr. Nazar

Your advertisement in the *Ottawa Citizen* for a Junior Environmental Officer precisely matches my qualifications. As a graduating student in Environmental Studies at Carleton University, I would like to apply for the position and have enclosed a resumé.

Beyond my specialist academic program, I have had relevant environmental field experience. For two summers, I worked with Professor Susan LeClerc in her studies of wetland pollution south of Georgian Bay, helping both in the laboratory and in the wetlands south of James Bay. I also enjoy and am used to the kind of outdoor work you require. In my first summer as a university student, I worked as a tree planter in harsh conditions in northern British Columbia. In addition, I am able to speak French well enough to converse with your French-speaking clients in Ontario and Quebec.

I would appreciate the chance to discuss with you further how I could contribute to Outlands Developments and will call you next week to see if it is convenient to arrange an interview.

Sincerely

Marco Garon

Electronic Applications

Increasingly, academic institutions and large employers are using online portfolio services such as Interfolio to manage applications. These services streamline the application process for both applicants and employers since they create application packages for each applicant that are easily viewable by the multiple members of a hiring or admissions committee or a management team. You can upload cover letters, official transcripts, standardized test results, CVs, writing samples, and portfolios. Referees can upload confidential letters of recommendation which are not viewable by the account holder, allowing them to send a single letter rather than one for each application. You can also upload individual cover letters, thereby avoiding the problem of sending a generic one.

However you approach online applications, it is advisable to save any documents in PDF format to ensure that your formatting is preserved.

Final Words of Advice

When you apply for a job, your application is likely to be one of many. This means that it must pass an initial screening process before it is considered seriously. For that reason, it is absolutely essential that you submit a package that looks professional. Your application package will be judged not just by what you say but also by how you say it. Take the time to double-check for grammar and spelling errors, and make sure that your documents are well formatted. With applications, as with job interviews, first impressions count.

Writing with Style

> **In this chapter, we will examine**
> - the importance of using clear diction and writing clear paragraphs;
> - strategies for making your writing both strong and concise; and
> - tips for developing a forceful, vigorous writing style.

Introduction

Writing with style does not mean inflating your prose with fancy words and extravagant images. Any style, from the simplest to the most elaborate, can be effective depending on the occasion and intent. Writers known for their style are those who have projected their own personality into their writing; we can hear a distinctive voice in what they say. Obviously it takes time to develop a unique style. To begin with, you have to decide what general effect you want to create.

Taste in style reflects the times. In earlier centuries, many respected writers wrote in an elaborate style that we would consider much too wordy. Today, journalists have led the trend toward short, easy-to-grasp sentences and paragraphs. Writing in an academic context, you may expect your audience to be more reflective than the average newspaper reader, but the most effective style is still one that is clear, concise, and forceful.

Be Clear

Use clear diction

A dictionary is a wise investment. It will help you understand unfamiliar words or archaic and technical senses of common words. Some dictionaries help you use words properly by offering example sentences that show how certain words are typically used. A dictionary will also help you with spelling. If you aren't sure if a particular word is too informal for your writing or if you have concerns that a certain word might be offensive, a good dictionary will give you this information.

You should be aware that Canadian usage and spelling may follow either British or American practice, but usually combines aspects of both. There are a number of Canadian dictionaries available today, including on-line dictionaries such as the *Canadian Oxford Dictionary Online,* that will help you to be consistent in your approach. It's also a good idea to make sure that the *language* feature of your word-processing program is set to *English (Canada).*

A thesaurus lists words that are closely related in meaning. It can help when you want to avoid repeating yourself or when you are fumbling for a word that's on the tip of your tongue. Your word-processing program also has a thesaurus feature that allows you to look up synonyms and antonyms easily. Be careful, though: make sure you distinguish between *denotative* and *connotative* meanings. A word's denotation is its primary or "dictionary" meaning. Its connotations are any associations that it may suggest; they may not be as exact as the denotations, but they are part of the impression the word conveys. If you examine a list of synonyms in a thesaurus, you will see that even words with similar meanings can have dramatically different connotations. For example, alongside the word *indifferent* your thesaurus may give the following: *neutral, aloof, callous, moderate, unenthusiastic, apathetic, unprejudiced,* and *fair.* Imagine the different impressions you would create if you chose one or the other of those words to complete this sentence: "Questioned about the experiment's chance of success, he was _____ in his response." In order to write clearly, you must remember that a reader may react to the suggestive meaning of a word as much as to its "dictionary" meaning.

Use plain English

Plain words are almost always more forceful than fancy ones. If you aren't sure what plain English is, think of the way you talk to your friends (apart from swearing and slang). Many of our most common words—the ones that sound most natural and direct—are short. A good number of them are also among the oldest words in the English language. By contrast, most of the words that English has derived from other languages are longer and more complicated; even those that have been used for centuries can sound artificial. For this reason you should beware of words loaded with prefixes (*pre-*, *post-*, *anti-*, *pro-*, *sub-*, *maxi-*, etc.) and suffixes (*-ate*, *-ize*, *-tion*, etc.). These Latinate attachments can make individual words more precise and efficient, but putting a lot of them together will make your writing seem dense and hard to understand. In many cases you can substitute a plain word for a fancy one:

Fancy	*Plain*
accomplish	do
cognizant	aware
commence	begin, start
conclusion	end
determinant	cause
fabricate	build
finalize	finish, complete
firstly	first
infuriate	anger
maximization	increase
modification	change
numerous	many
obviate	prevent
oration	speech
prioritize	rank
remuneration	pay
requisite	needed
sanitize	clean
subsequently	later
systematize	order
terminate	end
transpire	happen
utilize	use

Suggesting that you write in plain English does not mean that you should never pick an unfamiliar word or foreign derivative; sometimes those words are the only ones that will convey precisely what you mean. Inserting an unusual expression into a passage of plain writing can also be an effective means of catching the reader's attention—as long as you don't do it too often.

Avoid fancy jargon

All academic subjects have their own terminology; it may be unfamiliar to outsiders, but it helps specialists explain things to each other. The trouble is that
people sometimes use *jargon*—special, technical language—unnecessarily,
thinking it will make them seem more knowledgeable. Too often the result is
not clarity but complication. The principle is easy: use specialized terminology only when it's a kind of shorthand that will help you explain something
more precisely and efficiently. If plain prose will do just as well, stick to it.

Be precise

Always be as specific as you can. Avoid all-purpose adjectives like *major, significant*, and *important* and vague verbs such as *involve, entail*, and *exist* when
you can be more specific:

> *orig.*   Donald Smith was involved in the construction of the CPR.
>
> *rev.*   Donald Smith helped finance the construction of the CPR.

Here's another example:

> *orig.*   The Canada–US Free Trade Agreement was a significant legacy of
> Brian Mulroney's years as prime minister.
>
> *rev.*   The Canada–US Free Trade Agreement was a costly legacy of Brian
> Mulroney's years as prime minister.

(or)

> *rev.*   The Canada–US Free Trade Agreement was a beneficial legacy of
> Brian Mulroney's years as prime minister.

Avoid unnecessary qualifiers

Qualifiers such as *very, rather*, and *extremely* are overused. Saying that something is *very beautiful* may have less impact than saying simply that it is
beautiful. For example, compare these sentences:

> That is a beautiful garden.
>
> That is an extremely beautiful garden.

Which has more impact? When you think that an adjective needs qualifying—and sometimes it will—first see if it's possible to change either the adjective or the phrasing. Instead of writing

Multinational Drugs made a <u>very big</u> profit last year,

write a precise statement:

Multinational Drugs made an <u>unprecedented</u> profit last year,

or (if you aren't sure whether or not the profit actually set a record):

Multinational Drugs had a profit <u>increase of 40 per cent</u> last year.

In some cases, qualifiers not only weaken your writing but are redundant because the adjectives themselves are absolutes. To say that something is *very unique* makes as little sense as saying that someone is *slightly pregnant* or *extremely dead*.

Create clear paragraphs

Paragraphs come in so many sizes and patterns that no single formula could possibly cover them all. The two basic principles to remember are these:

1. a paragraph is a means of developing and framing an idea or impression; and
2. the divisions between paragraphs aren't random but indicate a shift in focus.

Develop your ideas

You are not likely to sit down and consciously ask yourself, "What pattern shall I use to develop this paragraph?" What comes first is the idea you intend to develop; the structure of the paragraph should flow from the idea itself and the way you want to discuss or expand it.

You may take one or several paragraphs to develop an idea fully. For a definition alone you could write 1 paragraph or 10, depending on the complexity of the subject and the nature of the assignment. Just remember that ideas need development, and that each new paragraph signals a change of ideas.

Consider the topic sentence

Skilled skim readers know that they can get the general drift of a book simply by reading the first sentence of each paragraph. The reason is that most paragraphs begin by stating the central idea to be developed. If you are writing your essay from a formal plan, you will probably find that each section and subsection will generate the topic sentence for a new paragraph.

Like the thesis statement for the essay as a whole, the topic sentence is not obligatory; in some paragraphs the controlling idea is not stated until the middle or even the end, and in others it is not stated at all but merely implied. Nevertheless, it's a good idea to think out a topic sentence for every paragraph. That way you'll be sure that each one has a readily graspable point and is clearly connected to what comes before and after. When revising your initial draft, check to see that each paragraph is held together by a topic sentence, either stated or implied. If you find that you can't formulate one, you should probably rework the whole paragraph.

Maintain focus

A clear paragraph should contain only those details that are in some way related to the central idea. It should also be structured so that the details are easily *seen* to be related. One way of showing these relationships is to keep the same grammatical subject in most of the sentences that make up the paragraph. When the grammatical subject keeps shifting, a paragraph loses focus, as in the following example:[1]

> *orig.* Students play a variety of sports these days. In the fall, football and field hockey still attract many, although an increasing number now play soccer. For some, basketball is the favourite when the fall season is over, but you will find that swimming, volleyball, and gymnastics are also popular. Cold winter temperatures bring hockey, skating, and skiing. In spring, students take up soccer again, while track and field, baseball, and tennis also attract many participants.

Here the grammatical subject (underlined) changes from sentence to sentence. Notice how much stronger the focus becomes when all the sentences have the same grammatical subject—either the same noun, a synonym, or a related pronoun:

> *rev.*   <u>Students</u> play a variety of sports these days. In the fall, <u>many</u> still choose football and field hockey, although an increasing <u>number</u> now play soccer. When the fall season is over, <u>some</u> turn to basketball; <u>others</u> prefer swimming, volleyball, or gymnastics. In cold winter temperatures many <u>students</u> enjoy hockey, skating, and skiing. In spring, <u>some</u> take up soccer again, while <u>others</u> choose track and field, baseball, or tennis.

Naturally it's not always possible to retain the same grammatical subject throughout a paragraph. If you were comparing the athletic pursuits of boys and girls, for example, you would have to switch back and forth between boys and girls as your grammatical subject. In the same way, you have to shift when you are discussing examples of an idea or exceptions to it.

Avoid monotony

If most or all of the sentences in your paragraph have the same grammatical subject, how do you avoid boring your reader? There are two easy ways:

1. **Use substitute words.** Pronouns, either personal (*I, we, you, he, she, it, they*) or demonstrative (*this, that, those*), can replace the subject, as can synonyms (words or phrases that mean the same thing). The revised paragraph on student athletics, for example, uses the pronouns *some, many,* and *others* as substitutes for students. Most well-written paragraphs have a liberal sprinkling of these substitute words.
2. **"Bury" the subject by putting something in front of it.** When the subject is placed in the middle of the sentence rather than at the beginning, it's less obvious to the reader. If you take another look at the revised paragraph, you'll see that in several sentences there is a word or phrase in front of the subject. Even a single word, such as *first, then, lately,* or *moreover,* will do the trick.

Link your ideas

To create coherent paragraphs, you need to link your ideas clearly. Linking words are those connectors—conjunctions and conjunctive adverbs—that show the relationship between one sentence, or part of a sentence, and another.

They're also known as transition words, because they form a bridge from one thought to another. Make a habit of using linking words when you shift from one grammatical subject or idea to the next, whether the shift occurs within a single paragraph or as you move from one paragraph to another. The following are some of the most common connectors and the logical relations they indicate:

Linking word	Logical relation
and also again furthermore in addition likewise moreover similarly	addition to previous idea
alternatively although but by contrast despite, in spite of even so however nevertheless on the other hand rather yet	change from previous idea
accordingly as a result consequently hence for this reason so therefore thus	summary or conclusion

Numerical terms such as *first, second,* and *third* also work well as links.

Vary paragraph length, but avoid extremes

Ideally, academic writing will have a balance of long and short paragraphs. However, it's best to avoid the extremes—especially the one-sentence paragraph, which can only state an idea without explaining or developing it. A series of very short paragraphs is usually a sign that you have not developed your ideas in enough detail or that you have started new paragraphs unnecessarily. On the other hand, a succession of long paragraphs can be difficult to read. In deciding when to start a new paragraph, consider what is clearest and most helpful for the reader.

Be Concise

At one time or another, you will probably be tempted to pad your writing. Whatever the reason—because you need to write 2000 or 3000 words and have only enough to say for 1000, or because you think length is strength and hope to get a better mark for the extra words—padding is a mistake.

Strong writing is always concise. It leaves out anything that does not serve some communicative or stylistic purpose, and it says as much as possible in as few words as possible. Concise writing will help you do better on both your essays and your exams.

Use adverbs and adjectives sparingly

Don't sprinkle adverbs and adjectives everywhere and don't use combinations of modifiers unless you are sure they clarify your meaning. One well-chosen word is always better than a series of synonyms:

> *orig.* As well as being <u>costly</u> and <u>financially extravagant</u>, the venture is <u>reckless</u> and <u>risky</u>.

> *rev.* The venture is <u>risky</u> as well as <u>costly</u>.

Avoid noun clusters

A recent trend in some writing is to use nouns as adjectives (as in the phrase *noun cluster*). This device can be effective occasionally, but frequent use can produce a monstrous pile of nouns. Breaking up noun clusters may not always result in fewer words, but it will make your writing easier to read:

> *orig.* insurance plan revision summary
>
> *rev.* summary of the revised insurance plan

Avoid chains of relative clauses

Sentences full of clauses beginning with *which*, *that*, or *who* are usually wordier than necessary. Try reducing some of those clauses to phrases or single words:

> *orig.* The solutions that were discussed last night have a practical benefit, which is easily grasped by people who have no technical training.
>
> *rev.* The solutions discussed last night have a practical benefit, easily grasped by non-technical people.

Try reducing clauses to phrases or words

Independent clauses can often be reduced by subordination. Here are a few examples:

> *orig.* The report was written in a clear and concise manner, and it was widely read.
>
> *rev.* Written in a clear and concise manner, the report was widely read.
>
> *rev.* Clear and concise, the report was widely read.
>
> *orig.* His plan was of a radical nature and was a source of embarrassment to his employer.
>
> *rev.* His radical plan embarrassed his employer.

Eliminate clichés and circumlocutions

Trite or roundabout phrases may flow from your pen automatically, but they make for stale prose. Unnecessary words are deadwood; be prepared to slash ruthlessly to keep your writing vital:

Wordy	*Revised*
due to the fact that	because
at this point in time	now

consensus of opinion	consensus
in the near future	soon
when all is said and done	[omit]
in the eventuality that	if
in all likelihood	likely
it could be said that	possibly, maybe
in all probability	probably
at the end of the day	ultimately, finally

Avoid "it is" and "there is" beginnings

Although it may not always be possible, try to avoid beginning sentences with *It is* . . . or *There is (are)* . . . Your sentences will be crisper and more concise:

orig. There is little time remaining for the sales manager to reverse the financial trend.

rev. Little time remains for the sales manager to reverse the financial trend.

Be Forceful

Developing a forceful, vigorous style simply means learning some common tricks of the trade and practising them until they become habit.

Choose active over passive verbs

An active verb creates more energy than a passive one does:

Active: She threw the ball.

Passive: The ball was thrown by her.

Moreover, passive constructions tend to produce awkward, convoluted phrasing. Writers of bureaucratic documents are among the worst offenders:

orig. It has been decided that the utilization of small rivers in the province for purposes of generating hydroelectric power should be studied by our department and that a report to the deputy should be made by our director as soon as possible.

The passive verbs in this mouthful make it hard to tell who is doing what. Passive verbs are appropriate in four cases:

1. When the subject is the passive recipient of some action:

   The cabinet minister was heckled by the angry crowd.

2. When you want to emphasize the object rather than the person acting:

   The antipollution devices in all three plants will be improved.

3. When you want to avoid an awkward shift from one subject to another in a sentence or paragraph:

   The Jesuits began to convert the Hurons but were attacked by the Iroquois band before they had completed the mission.

4. When you want to avoid placing responsibility or blame:

   Several errors were made in the calculations.

When these exceptions don't apply, make an effort to use active verbs for a livelier style.

Use personal subjects

Most of us find it more interesting to learn about people than about things. Wherever possible, therefore, make the subjects of your sentences personal. This trick goes hand in hand with the use of active verbs. Almost any sentence becomes livelier with active verbs and a personal subject:

orig. The outcome of the union members' vote was the decision to resume work on Monday.

rev. The union members voted to return to work on Monday.

Here's another example:

orig. It can be assumed that an agreement was reached, since there were smiles on both management and union sides when the meeting was concluded.

rev. We can assume that management and the union reached an agreement, since both sides were smiling when they concluded the meeting.

(or)

rev.   Apparently <u>management and the union reached</u> an agreement, since <u>both sides were smiling</u> when <u>they concluded</u> the meeting.

Use concrete details

Concrete details are easier to understand—and to remember—than abstract theories. Whenever you are discussing abstract concepts, therefore, always provide specific examples and illustrations; if you have a choice between a concrete word and an abstract one, choose the concrete. Consider this sentence:

> The French explored the northern territory and traded with the Aboriginal people.

Now see how a few specific details can bring the facts to life:

> The French voyageurs paddled their way along the river systems of the North, trading their blankets and copper kettles with the Aboriginal people for furs.

Adding concrete details doesn't mean getting rid of all abstractions. Just try to find the proper balance. The above example is one instance where adding words, if they are concrete and correct, can improve your writing.

Make important ideas stand out

Experienced writers know how to manipulate sentences in order to emphasize certain points. The following are some of their techniques.

Place key words in strategic positions

The positions of emphasis in a sentence are the beginning and, above all, the end. If you want to bring your point home with force, don't put the key words in the middle of the sentence. Save them for the end:

orig.   People are less afraid of losing wealth than of losing face in this image-conscious society.

rev.   In this image-conscious society, people are less afraid of losing wealth than of losing face.

Subordinate minor ideas

Small children connect incidents with a string of *ands*, as if everything were of equal importance:

> Our bus was delayed, and we were late for school, and we missed the test.

As they grow up, however, they learn to *subordinate*—that is, to make one part of a sentence less important in order to emphasize another point:

> Because the bus was delayed, we were late and missed the test.

Major ideas stand out more and connections become clearer when minor ideas are subordinated:

> *orig.*   Night came and the ship slipped away from her captors.
>
> *rev.*   When night came, the ship slipped away from her captors.

Make your most important idea the subject of the main clause, and try to put it at the end, where it will be most emphatic:

> *orig.*   I was relieved when I saw my marks.
>
> *rev.*   When I saw my marks, I was relieved.

Vary sentence structure

As with anything else, variety adds spice to writing. One way of adding variety which will also make an important idea stand out is to use a periodic rather than a simple sentence structure.

Most sentences follow the simple pattern of subject–verb–object (plus modifiers):

> The premier lost the election.
>   s   v   o

A *simple sentence* such as this gives the main idea at the beginning and therefore creates little tension. A *periodic sentence*, on the other hand, does not give the main clause until the end, after one or more subordinate clauses:

Since the premier had failed to keep her promises or to inspire the voters, in the next election <u>she</u> <u>lost badly</u>.
                                    S   V

The longer the periodic sentence is, the greater the suspense and the more emphatic the final part. Since this high-tension structure is more difficult to read than the simple sentence, your reader would be exhausted if you used it too often. Save it for those times when you want to make a very strong point.

Vary sentence length

A short sentence can add impact to an important point, especially when it comes after a series of longer sentences. This technique can be particularly useful for conclusions. Don't overdo it, though—a string of long sentences may be monotonous, but a string of short ones can make your writing sound like a children's book.

Still, academic papers usually have too many long sentences rather than too many short ones. Since short sentences are easier to read, try breaking up clusters of long ones. Check any sentence of more than 20 words or so to see if it will benefit from being split.

Use contrast

Just as a jeweller highlights a diamond by displaying it against dark velvet, so you can highlight an idea by placing it against a contrasting background:

> *orig.* Most employees in industry do not have indexed pensions.
>
> *rev.* <u>Unlike civil servants</u>, most employees in industry do not have indexed pensions.

Using parallel phrasing will increase the effect of the contrast:

> Although <u>she often spoke</u> to business groups, <u>she seldom spoke</u> in Parliament.

Use a well-placed adverb or correlative construction

Adding an adverb or two can sometimes help you dramatize a concept:

> *orig.* Although I dislike the proposal, I must accept it as the practical answer.
>
> *rev.* Although <u>emotionally</u> I dislike the concept, <u>intellectually</u> I must accept it as the practical answer.

Correlatives such as *both . . . and* or *not only . . . but also* can be used to emphasize combinations as well:

orig.   Professor Nderu was a good instructor and a good friend.

rev.   Professor Nderu was <u>both</u> a good instructor <u>and</u> a good friend.

(or)

rev.   Professor Nderu was <u>not only</u> a good instructor <u>but also</u> a good friend.

Use repetition

Repetition is a highly effective device for adding emphasis:

<u>He fought</u> injustice and corruption. <u>He fought</u> complacent politicians and inept policies. <u>He fought</u> hard, but <u>he</u> always <u>fought</u> fairly.

Of course, you would only use such a dramatic technique on rare occasions.

Some Final Advice

Write before you revise

No one expects you to sit down and put all this advice into practice as soon as you start to write. You would feel so constrained that it would be hard to get anything down on paper at all. You will be better off if you begin concentrating on these guidelines during the final stages of the writing process when you are looking critically at what you have already written. Some experienced writers can combine the creative and critical functions, but most of us find it easier to write a rough draft first before starting the detailed task of revising and editing.

Use your ears

Your ears are probably your best critics; make good use of them. Before producing a final copy of any piece of writing, read it out loud in a clear voice. The difference between cumbersome and fluent passages will be unmistakable.

Note

1.   Discussion of focus based on Robert Cluett and Lee Ahlborn, *Effective English Prose: Writing for Meaning, Reading for Style* (New York: L.W. Singer, 1965), 51.

Common Errors in Grammar and Usage

In this chapter, we will examine

- common errors in grammar and usage;
- strategies for identifying errors in your writing; and
- techniques for avoiding or correcting errors in grammar and usage.

Introduction

This chapter is not a comprehensive grammar lesson; it's simply a survey of those areas where students most often make mistakes. It will help you pinpoint weaknesses as you edit your work. Once you get into the habit of checking your work, it won't be long before you are correcting potential problems as you write.

The grammatical terms used here are the most basic and familiar ones; if you need to review some of them, see Chapter 13 or the Glossary. If you're interested in a more exhaustive treatment, consult one of the many books that deal exclusively with grammar and usage.

Sentence Unity

Sentence fragments

To be complete, a sentence must have both a subject and a verb in an independent clause; if it doesn't, it's a fragment. There are times in informal writing when it is acceptable to use a sentence fragment in order to give emphasis to a point:

✓ Will the government try to abolish the Senate? Not likely.

Here the sentence fragment *Not likely* is clearly intended to be understood as a short form of *It is not likely that it will try.* Unintentional sentence fragments, on the other hand, usually seem incomplete rather than shortened:

> ✗   I enjoy living in Vancouver. <u>Being a skier who likes the sea.</u>

The last "sentence" is incomplete because it lacks an independent clause with a subject and a verb. (Remember that a participle such as *being* is a *verbal*, or "part-verb," not a verb.) The fragment can be made into a complete sentence by adding a subject and a verb:

> ✓   I <u>am</u> a skier who likes the sea.

Alternatively, you could join the fragment to the preceding sentence:

> ✓   Being a skier who likes the sea, I enjoy living in Vancouver.

> ✓   I enjoy living in Vancouver, since I am a skier who likes the sea.

Run-on sentences

A run-on sentence is one that continues beyond the point where it should have stopped:

> ✗   Mosquitoes and blackflies are annoying, but they don't stop tourists from coming to spend their holidays in Canada, and such is the case in Ontario's northland.

This run-on sentence could be fixed by removing the word *and* and adding a period or semicolon after *Canada.*

Another kind of run-on sentence is one in which two independent clauses are wrongly joined by a comma. An independent clause is a phrase that can stand by itself as a complete sentence. Two independent clauses should not be joined by a comma without a coordinating conjunction:

> ✗   Northrop Frye won international acclaim as a critic, he was an English professor at the University of Toronto.

This error is known as a *comma splice*. There are three ways of correcting it:

1. by putting a period after *critic* and starting a new sentence:

    ✓ . . . as a critic. He . . .

2. by replacing the comma with a semicolon:

    ✓ . . . as a critic; he . . .

3. by making one of the independent clauses subordinate to the other, so that it doesn't stand by itself:

    ✓ Northrop Frye, who won international acclaim as a critic, was an English professor at the University of Toronto.

The one exception to the rule that independent clauses cannot be joined by a comma arises when the clauses are very short and arranged in a tight sequence:

    ✓ I opened the door, I saw the skunk, and I closed the door.

You should not use this kind of sentence very often.

Contrary to what many people think, words such as *however*, *therefore*, and *thus* cannot be used to join independent clauses:

    ✗ Two of my friends started out studying commerce, however they quickly decided they didn't like accounting.

This mistake can be corrected by beginning a new sentence after *commerce* or (preferably) by replacing the comma with a semicolon:

    ✓ Two of my friends started out studying commerce; however, they quickly decided they didn't like accounting.

Another option is to join the two independent clauses with a coordinating conjunction—*and, or, nor, but, for, yet, so*, or *whereas*:

    ✓ Two of my friends started out studying commerce, but they quickly decided they didn't like accounting.

Faulty predication

When the subject of a sentence is not grammatically connected to what follows (the predicate), the result is faulty predication:

✗ The <u>reason</u> he failed <u>was because</u> he couldn't handle multiple-choice exams.

The problem with this sentence is that *reason* and *was because* mean essentially the same thing. The subject is a noun and the verb *was* needs a noun clause to complete it:

✓ The <u>reason</u> he failed <u>was that</u> he couldn't handle multiple-choice exams.

Another solution is to rephrase the sentence:

✓ He failed because he couldn't handle multiple-choice exams.

Faulty predication also occurs with *is when* and *is where* constructions:

✗ The climax <u>is when</u> the servant discovers the body.

Again, you can correct this error in one of two ways:

1. Follow the *is* with a noun phrase to complete the sentence:

    ✓ The climax <u>is the discovery</u> of the body by the servant.

    (or)

    ✓ The climax <u>is the servant's discovery</u> of the body.

2. Change the verb:

    ✓ The climax <u>occurs</u> when the servant discovers the body.

Subject–Verb Agreement

Identifying the subject

A verb should always agree in number with its subject. Sometimes, however, when the subject does not come at the beginning of the sentence or when it is separated from the verb by other information, you may be tempted to use a verb form that does not agree:

> ✗   The increase in the rate for freight and passengers were condemned by the farmers.

The subject here is *increase*, not *freight and passengers*; therefore, the verb should be singular:

> ✓   The increase in the rate for freight and passengers was condemned by the farmers.

Either, neither, each

The indefinite pronouns *either*, *neither*, and *each* always take singular verbs:

> ✓   Neither of the defendants has a trial date.

> ✓   Each of them has a lawyer.

Compound subjects

When *or*, *either . . . or*, or *neither . . . nor* is used to create a compound subject, the verb should usually agree with the last item in the subject:

> ✓   Neither the professor nor her students were able to solve the equation.

> ✓   Either the students or the TA was misinformed.

You may find, however, that it sounds awkward in some cases to use a singular verb when a singular item follows a plural item:

> *orig.*   Either my history books or my biology text is going to gather dust this weekend.

In such instances, it's better to rephrase the sentence:

> *rev.*   This weekend, I'm going to ignore either my history books or my biology text.

Unlike the word *and*, which creates a compound subject and therefore takes a plural verb, the phrases *as well as* and *in addition to* do not create compound subjects; therefore the verb remains singular:

✓ Tourtière and sugar pie are traditional Quebec dishes.

✓ Tourtière, as well as sugar pie, is a traditional Quebec dish.

Collective nouns

A collective noun is a singular noun that comprises a number of members, such as *family*, *army*, or *team*. If the noun refers to the members as one unit, it takes a singular verb:

✓ The team is playing its first game tonight.

If, in the context of the sentence, the noun refers to the members as individuals, the verb becomes plural:

✓ The team are receiving their sweaters before the game.

✓ The majority of immigrants to Canada settle in cities.

Titles

The title of a book or a movie or the name of a business or organization is always treated as a singular noun, even if it contains plural words; therefore, it takes a singular verb:

✓ *Tales of the South Pacific* was a bestseller.

✓ Goodman & Goodman is handling the legal dispute.

Verb Tenses

Native speakers of English usually know without thinking which verb tense to use in a given context. However, a few tenses can be confusing.

The past perfect

If the main verb is in the past tense and you want to refer to something that happened before that time, use the *past perfect* (*had* followed by the past participle). The time sequence will not be clear if you use the simple past in both clauses:

✗ He <u>hoped</u> that she <u>fixed</u> the printer.

✓ He <u>hoped</u> that she <u>had fixed</u> the printer.

Similarly, when you are reporting what someone said in the past—that is, when you are using *past indirect discourse*—you should use the past perfect tense in the clause describing what was said:

✗ He <u>told</u> the TA that he <u>wrote</u> the essay that week.

✓ He <u>told</u> the TA that he <u>had written</u> the essay that week.

Using "if"

When you are describing a possibility in the future, use the present tense in the condition (*if*) clause and the future tense in the consequence clause:

✓ If he <u>tests</u> us on French verbs, I <u>will fail</u>.

When the possibility is unlikely, it is conventional—especially in formal writing—to use the *subjunctive* in the *if* clause, and *would* followed by the base verb in the consequence clause:

✓ If he <u>were</u> to cancel the test, I <u>would cheer</u>.

When you are describing a hypothetical instance in the past, use the *past subjunctive* (it has the same form as the past perfect) in the *if* clause and *would have* followed by the past participle for the consequence. A common error is to use *would have* in both clauses:

✗ If he <u>would have been</u> friendlier, I <u>would have asked</u> him to be my lab partner.

✓ If he <u>had been</u> friendlier, I <u>would have asked</u> him to be my lab partner.

Writing about literature

When you are describing a literary work in its historical context, use the past tense:

✓ Margaret Atwood <u>wrote</u> *Surfacing* at a time when George Grant's *Technology and Empire* <u>was persuading</u> people to reassess techno-cratic values.

To discuss what goes on within a work of literature, however, you should use the present tense:

> ✓ The narrator <u>retreats</u> to the woods and <u>tries</u> to escape the rationalism of her father's world.

When you are discussing an episode or incident in a literary work and want to refer to a prior incident or a future one, use past or future tenses accordingly:

> ✓ The narrator <u>returns</u> to northern Quebec, where she <u>spent</u> her summers as a child; by the time she <u>leaves</u>, she <u>will have rediscovered</u> herself.

Be sure to return to the present tense when you have finished referring to events in the past or future.

Pronouns

Pronoun reference

The link between a pronoun and the noun it refers to must be clear. If the noun doesn't appear in the same sentence as the pronoun, it should appear in the preceding sentence:

> ✗ The <u>textbook supply</u> in the bookstore had run out, so we borrowed <u>them</u> from the library.

Since *textbook* is used as an adjective rather than a noun, it cannot serve as referent or antecedent for the pronoun *them*. You must either replace *them* or change the phrase *textbook supply*:

> ✓ The <u>textbook supply</u> in the bookstore had run out, so we borrowed <u>the texts</u> from the library.

> ✓ The bookstore had run out of <u>textbooks</u>, so we borrowed <u>them</u> from the library.

When a sentence contains more than one noun, make sure there is no ambiguity about which noun the pronoun refers to:

✗ The public wants better <u>social services</u> along with lower <u>taxes</u>, but the government does not favour <u>them</u>.

What does the pronoun *them* refer to: the taxes, the social services, or both?

✓ The public wants better <u>social services</u> along with lower taxes, but the government does not advocate <u>spending increases</u>.

Using "it" and "this"

Using *it* and *this* without a clear referent can lead to confusion:

✗ Although the directors wanted to meet in January, <u>it (this)</u> didn't take place until May.

✓ Although the directors wanted to meet in January, <u>the conference</u> didn't take place until May.

Make sure that *it* or *this* clearly refers to a specific noun or pronoun.

Using "one"

People often use the word *one* to avoid overusing *I* in their writing. Although in Britain this is common, in Canada and the United States frequent use of *one* may seem too formal and even a bit pompous:

orig. If <u>one</u> were to apply for the grant, <u>one</u> would find <u>oneself</u> engulfed in so many bureaucratic forms that <u>one's</u> patience would be stretched thin.

While there is nothing grammatically incorrect in this example, it may strike the reader as stiff or pretentious. The best thing to do is to recast the sentence with a plural subject:

rev. If <u>researchers</u> were to apply for grants, <u>they</u> would find <u>themselves</u> engulfed in so many bureaucratic forms that <u>their</u> patience would be stretched thin.

Use *one* sparingly, and don't be afraid of the occasional *I*. Just remember not to mix the third person *one* with the second person *you*:

> ✕ When <u>one</u> visits the Rockies, <u>you</u> are impressed by the grandeur of the scenery.

Using "me" and other objective pronouns

Remembering that it is wrong to say "Dorcas and me were invited to present our findings to the delegates" rather than "Dorcas and I were invited . . .", many people use the subjective form of the pronoun even when it should be objective:

> ✕ The delegates <u>invited</u> Dorcas and <u>I</u> to present our findings.

> ✓ The delegates <u>invited</u> Dorcas and <u>me</u> to present our findings.

The verb *invited* requires an object; *me* is the objective case. A good way to tell which form is correct is to ask yourself how the sentence would sound with only the pronoun. You will know by ear that the subjective form—"The delegates invited *I*"—is inappropriate.

The same problem often arises with prepositions, which should also be followed by a noun or pronoun in the objective case:

> ✕ <u>Between</u> you and <u>I</u>, this result doesn't make sense.

> ✓ <u>Between</u> you and <u>me</u>, this result doesn't make sense.

> ✕ Eating well is a problem <u>for we</u> students.

> ✓ Eating well is a problem <u>for us</u> students.

There are times, however, when the correct case can sound stiff or awkward:

> *orig.*   <u>To whom</u> was the award given?

Rather than using a correct but awkward form, try to reword the sentence:

> *rev.*   <u>Who received</u> the award?

Exceptions for pronouns following prepositions

The rule that a pronoun following a preposition takes the objective case has exceptions. When the preposition is followed by a clause, the pronoun should take the case required by its position in the clause:

✗ The students showed some concern <u>over</u> <u>whom</u> <u>would be selected</u> as Dean.

Although the pronoun follows the preposition *over*, it is also the subject of the verb *would be selected* and therefore requires the subjective case:

✓ The students showed some concern <u>over</u> <u>who</u> <u>would be selected</u> as Dean.

Similarly, when a *gerund* (a word that acts partly as a noun and partly as a verb) is the subject of a clause, the pronoun that modifies it takes the possessive case:

✗ We were surprised <u>by</u> <u>him</u> <u>dropping</u> out of school.

✓ We were surprised <u>by</u> <u>his</u> <u>dropping</u> out of school.

✗ He was tired <u>of</u> <u>me</u> <u>reminding</u> him.

✓ He was tired <u>of</u> <u>my</u> <u>reminding</u> him.

Modifiers

Adjectives modify nouns; adverbs modify verbs, adjectives, and other adverbs. Do not use an adjective to modify a verb:

✗ He played <u>good</u>. (adjective with verb)

✓ He played <u>well</u>. (adverb modifying verb)

✓ He played <u>really</u> <u>well</u>. (adverb modifying adverb)

✓ He had a <u>good</u> style. (adjective modifying noun)

✓ He had a <u>really</u> <u>good</u> style. (adverb modifying adjective)

Squinting modifiers

Remember that clarity depends largely on word order: to avoid confusion, the connections between the different parts of a sentence must be clear. Modifiers should therefore be as close as possible to the words they modify. A squinting modifier is one that, because of its position, seems to look in two directions at once:

✗ She expected <u>after the announcement</u> a decline in the stock market.

Was *after the announcement* the time of expectation or the time of the market decline? Changing the order of the sentence or rephrasing it will make the meaning clearer:

- ✓ After the announcement, she expected a decline in the stock market.

- ✓ She expected the stock market to decline after the announcement.

Other squinting modifiers can be corrected in the same way:

- ✗ Our English professor gave a lecture on *Beowulf*, which was well illustrated.

- ✓ Our English professor gave a well-illustrated lecture on *Beowulf*.

Often the modifier works best when placed immediately in front of the phrase it modifies. Notice the difference that this placement can make:

Only she guessed the motive for the theft.

She only guessed the motive for the theft.

She guessed only the motive for the theft.

She guessed the motive for the theft only.

Dangling modifiers

Modifiers that have no grammatical connection with anything else in the sentence are said to be dangling:

- ✗ Walking around the campus in June, the river and trees made a picturesque scene.

Who is doing the walking? Here's another example:

- ✗ Reflecting on the results of the poll, it was decided not to announce the new tax cuts right away.

Who is doing the reflecting? Clarify the meaning by connecting the dangling modifier to a new subject:

- ✓ Walking around the campus in June, Maryam thought the river and trees made a picturesque scene.

✓ <u>Reflecting</u> on the results of the poll, <u>the councillors</u> decided not to announce the new tax cuts right away.

Pairs and Parallels

Comparisons

Make sure that your comparisons are complete. The second element in a comparison should be equivalent to the first, whether the equivalence is stated or merely implied:

✗ Today's students have a greater understanding of calculus than their parents.

This sentence suggests that the two things being compared are *calculus* and *parents*. Adding a second verb (*have*) equivalent to the first one shows that the two things being compared are parents' understanding and students' understanding:

✓ Today's students <u>have</u> a greater understanding of calculus than their parents <u>have</u>.

A similar problem arises in the following comparison:

✗ That new text is <u>a boring book</u> and so are the lectures.

The lectures may be boring, but they are not a boring book; to make sense, the two parts of the comparison must be parallel:

✓ The new text is <u>boring</u> and so are the lectures.

Correlatives

Constructions such as *both . . . and, not only . . . but also,* and *neither . . . nor* are especially tricky. For the implied comparison to work, the two parts that come after the coordinating term must be grammatically equivalent:

✗ He <u>not only bakes</u> cakes <u>but also bread</u>.
✓ He bakes <u>not only cakes</u> <u>but also bread</u>.

Parallel phrasing

A series of items in a sentence should be phrased in parallel wording. Make sure that all the parts of a parallel construction are in fact equal:

✗ We had to turn in <u>our rough notes</u>, <u>our calculations</u>, and <u>finished assignment</u>.

✓ We had to turn in <u>our rough notes</u>, <u>our calculations</u>, and <u>our finished assignment</u>.

Once you have decided to include the pronoun *our* in the first two elements, the third must have it too.

For clarity as well as stylistic grace, keep similar ideas in similar form:

✗ He <u>failed</u> economics and <u>barely passed</u> statistics, but political science <u>was</u> a subject he did well in.

✓ He <u>failed</u> economics and barely <u>passed</u> statistics but <u>did well</u> in political science.

Faulty parallelism is a common problem in bulleted or numbered lists:

✗ There are several reasons for purchasing this model:
   - low <u>cost</u>
   - <u>there is</u> an instant rebate
   - <u>covered</u> by full one-year warranty
   - <u>getting</u> a free carrying case with your purchase

✓ There are several reasons for purchasing this model:
   - low <u>cost</u>
   - instant <u>rebate</u>
   - full one-year <u>warranty</u>
   - <u>carrying case</u>

Punctuation

> **In this chapter, we will examine**
> - the role of punctuation marks as the traffic signals of writing;
> - examples of common punctuation errors; and
> - techniques for avoiding or correcting errors in punctuation.

Introduction

Punctuation causes students so many problems that it deserves a chapter of its own. If your punctuation is faulty, your readers will be confused and may have to backtrack; worse still, they may be tempted to skip over the rough spots. Punctuation marks are the traffic signals of writing; use them with precision to keep readers moving smoothly through your work.

Items in this chapter are arranged alphabetically: *apostrophe, brackets, colon, comma, dash, ellipsis, exclamation mark, hyphen, italics, parentheses, period, quotation marks,* and *semicolon*.

Apostrophe [']

1. **Use an apostrophe to indicate possession**. The following rules are the easiest to remember:

   a. To illustrate the possessive, create an "of" phrase:

the Perkins house	→	the house <u>of the Perkins</u>
the girls fathers	→	the fathers <u>of the girls</u>
the childrens parents	→	the parents <u>of the children</u>
Shakespeares plays	→	the plays <u>of Shakespeare</u>

b. If the noun in the "of" phrase ends in "s", add an apostrophe:

> the Perkins' house
> the girls' fathers

c. If the noun in the "of" phrase does not end in "s", add an apostrophe plus "s":

> the children's parents
> Shakespeare's plays

2. **Use an apostrophe to show contractions of words:**

> isn't   we'll   he's   shouldn't   I'm

Caution: don't confuse *it's* (the contraction of *it is*) with *its* (the possessive of *it*), which has no apostrophe. And remember that possessive pronouns never take an apostrophe: *yours, hers, its, ours, yours, theirs.*

Brackets [ ]

Brackets are square enclosures, not to be confused with parentheses (which are round). **Use brackets to set off a remark of your own within a quotation.** The brackets indicate that the words enclosed are not those of the person quoted:

> Fox maintained, "Obstacles to Western unification [in the eighties] are as many as they are serious."

Brackets are sometimes used to enclose *sic*, which is used after an error such as a misspelling to show that the mistake was in the original. *Sic* may be italicized:

> The politician, in his letter to constituents, wrote about "these parlouse [*sic*] times of economic difficulty."

Colon [:]

A colon indicates that something is to follow.

1. **Use a colon before a formal statement or series:**

    ✔ The winners are the following: Anna, Dieter, George, and Hugh.

    Do not use a colon if the words preceding it do not form a complete sentence:

    ✘ The winners are: Anna, Dieter, George, and Hugh.

    ✔ The winners are Anna, Dieter, George, and Hugh.

    On the other hand, a colon often precedes a vertical list, even when the introductory part is not a complete sentence:

    ✔ The winners are: Anna Singh

    Dieter Goering

    George Merasty

    Hugh Mackay

2. **Use a colon for formality before a direct quotation or when a complete sentence precedes the quotation:**

    The leaders of the anti-nuclear group repeated their message: "The world needs bread before bombs."

3. **Use a colon between numbers expressing time and ratios:**

    4:30 p.m.
    The ratio of calcium to potassium should be 7:1.

Comma [,]

Commas are the trickiest of all punctuation marks; even the experts differ on when to use them. Most agree, however, that too many commas are as bad as too few since they make writing choppy and awkward to read. Certainly recent writers use fewer commas than earlier stylists did. Whenever you are in doubt, let clarity be your guide. The most widely accepted conventions are these:

1. **Use a comma to separate two independent clauses joined by a co-ordinating conjunction (*and, but, for, or, nor, yet, so, whereas*).** By signalling that there are two clauses, the comma will prevent the reader

from thinking that the beginning of the second clause is the end of
the first:

✗ He went out for dinner with his sister and his roommate joined
them later.

✓ He went out for dinner with his sister, and his roommate joined
them later.

When the second clause has the same subject as the first, you have
the option of omitting both the second subject and the comma:

✓ She can stickhandle well, but she can't shoot.

✓ She can stickhandle well but can't shoot.

If you mistakenly punctuate two sentences as if they were one,
the result will be a *run-on sentence*; if you use a comma but forget the
coordinating conjunction, the result will be a *comma splice*:

✗ We took the children to the zoo, it was closed for repairs.

✓ We took the children to the zoo, but it was closed for repairs.

Remember that words such as *however*, *therefore*, and *thus* are
conjunctive adverbs, not conjunctions; if you use one of them to
join two independent clauses, the result will again be a *comma splice*:

✗ She was accepted into medical school, however, she took a year
off to earn her tuition.

✓ She was accepted into medical school; however, she took a year
off to earn her tuition.

Conjunctive adverbs are often confused with conjunctions. You
can distinguish between the two if you remember that a conjunctive
adverb's position in a sentence can be changed:

✓ She was accepted into medical school; she took a year off, however, to earn her tuition.

The position of a conjunction, on the other hand, is invariable; it
must be placed between the two clauses:

✓ She was accepted into medical school, but she took a year off to
earn her tuition.

A good rule of thumb, then, is to *use a comma when the linking word can't move.*

When, in rare cases, the independent clauses are short and closely related, they may be joined by a comma alone:

✓ I came, I saw, I conquered.

2. **Use a comma between items in a series.** Place a coordinating conjunction before the last item:

✓ She finally found an apartment that was large, bright, and clean.

✓ Then she had to scrounge around for dishes, pots, cutlery, and a kettle.

The comma before the conjunction (known as the *serial comma* or *Oxford comma*) is optional for single items in a series:

✓ She kept a cat, a dog and a budgie.

✓ She kept a cat, a dog, and a budgie.

For phrases in a series, however, use the final comma to help to prevent confusion:

✗ When we set off on our trip, we were warned about passport thieves, attacks on single women and lost children.

In this case, a comma would prevent the reader from thinking that attacks were made on lost children as well as single women:

✓ We were warned about passport thieves, attacks on single women, and lost children.

3. **Use a comma to separate adjectives preceding a noun when they modify the same element:**

✓ It was a rainy, windy night.

However, when the adjectives do not modify the same element, you should not use a comma:

✗ It was a pleasant, winter outing.

Here *winter* modifies *outing*, but *pleasant* modifies the whole phrase *winter outing*. A good way of deciding whether or not you need a comma is to see if you can reverse the order of the adjectives. If you can reverse them (*rainy, windy night* or *windy, rainy night*), use a comma; if you can't (*winter pleasant outing*), omit the comma:

✓ It was a pleasant winter outing.

4. **Use commas to set off an interruption (or "parenthetical element"):**

✓ The film, I hear, isn't nearly as good as the book.

✓ The TA, however, couldn't answer the question.

Remember to put commas on both sides of the interruption:

✗ The TA however, couldn't answer the question.

✗ The music, they say was adapted from a piece by Mozart.

✓ The music, they say, was adapted from a piece by Mozart.

5. **Use commas to set off words or phrases that provide additional but non-essential information:**

✓ Our president, Sue Stephens, does her job well.

✓ The golden retriever, his closest companion, went with him everywhere.

In these examples, *Sue Stephens* and his *closest companion* are *appositives*: they give additional information about the nouns they refer to (*president* and *golden retriever*), but the sentences would make sense without them. Here's another example:

✓ My oldest friend, who lives in Halifax, was married last week.

The phrase *who lives in Halifax* is a *non-restrictive modifier* because it does not limit the meaning of the word it modifies (*friend*). Without that modifying clause the sentence would still specify who was married. Since the information the clause provides is not necessary to the meaning of the sentence, you must use commas on both sides to set it off.

In contrast, a *restrictive modifier* is one that provides essential information; it must not be set apart from the element it modifies, and commas should not be used:

✓ The man who came to dinner was my uncle.

Without the clause *who came to dinner*, the reader would not know which man was the uncle.

To avoid confusion, be sure to distinguish carefully between essential and additional information. The difference can be important:

> Students, who are unwilling to work, should not receive grants. (All students are unwilling to work and should not receive grants.)

> Students who are unwilling to work should not receive grants. (Only those who are unwilling to work should be denied grants.)

6. **Use a comma after an introductory phrase when omitting it would cause confusion:**

✗ On the balcony above the singers entertained the diners.

✓ On the balcony above, the singers entertained the diners.

✗ When he turned away the prisoner disappeared.

✓ When he turned away, the prisoner disappeared.

7. **Use a comma to separate elements in dates and addresses:**

> February 2, 2012 (Commas are often omitted if the day comes first: 2 February 2012.)

> 117 Hudson Drive, Edmonton, Alberta

> They lived in Dartmouth, Nova Scotia.

8. **Use a comma before a quotation in a sentence:**

> He said, "Life is too short to worry."

> "The children's safety," he warned, "is in your hands."

For more formality, or if the quotation is preceded by a complete sentence, you may use a colon (see pages 168–9).

9. **Use a comma with a name followed by a title:**

> David Gunn, President

> Patrice Lareau, M.D.

10. **Do not use a comma between a subject and its verb:**

✗ Her favourite flavour of all, is vanilla.

✓ Her favourite flavour of all is vanilla.

11. **Do not use a comma between a verb and its object:**

✗ He immediately decided, what he must do.

✓ He immediately decided what he must do.

12. **Do not use a comma between a coordinating conjunction and the following clause:**

✗ Ellen got honours but, Daniel failed the course.

✓ Ellen got honours, but Daniel failed the course.

Dash [—]

A dash (also called an *em dash* because it's about the same width as a capital letter *m*) creates an abrupt pause, emphasizing the words that follow. Never use dashes as casual substitutes for other punctuation; overuse can detract from the calm, well-reasoned effect you want to create.

1. **Use a dash to stress a word or phrase:**

The British—as a matter of honour—vowed to retake the islands.

Ramirez was well received in the legislature—at first.

2. **Use a dash in interrupted or unfinished dialogue:**

"But I thought—" Donald tried to explain, but Mario cut him off with a wave of his hand.

You can type two hyphens together, with no spaces on either side, to show a dash; your word processor may automatically convert this to a solid line as you continue typing. Alternatively, you can insert an em dash from the list of special characters in your word-processing program.

En Dash [–]

An en dash is shorter than a full dash and slightly longer than a hyphen, approximately the width of a capital letter *n*. It denotes that there is a range from one thing to another.

Use an en dash rather than a hyphen to separate parts of inclusive numbers or dates:

> The years 1890–1914
>
> pages 3–10

See pages 176–7 for guidelines on when to use a hyphen.

Ellipsis [. . .]

1. **Use an ellipsis (three dots) to show an omission from a quotation:**

   For an ellipsis within a sentence, use three periods with a space before each and a space after the last:

   > "The committee reported that medical tests . . . verified that alcohol was a factor in the fatal accident."

   If the omission comes at the beginning of the quotation, an ellipsis is not necessarily used:

   > The defense lawyer cited evidence that "verified that alcohol was a factor in the accident."

   When the omission comes at the end of a sentence, use four periods with no space before the first or after the last:

   > The judge noted that "alcohol was a factor. . . ."

   To omit a full line of a poem, use a full line of periods:

   > Cedar and jagged fir
   >
   > . . . .
   >
   > against the gray
   >
   > and cloud-piled sky

2. **Use an ellipsis to show that a series of numbers continues indefinitely:**

> 1, 3, 5, 7, 9 . . .

Exclamation Mark [!]

An exclamation mark helps to show emotion or feeling. It is usually found in dialogue:

> "Woe is me!" she cried.

In academic writing, you should use it only in those rare cases when you want to give a point emotional emphasis:

> He predicted that there would be zero inflation this year. Some forecast!

Hyphen [-]

1. **Use a hyphen if you must divide a word at the end of a line.** The default setting in most word-processing programs will wrap text to a new line if a word is too long to fit on one line. However, there are instances—for example, when you're formatting text in narrow columns—when hyphenation might be preferred. If that is the case, turn on the automatic hyphenation feature in your word-processing program and it will make any word-division decisions for you.

2. **Use a hyphen to separate the parts of certain compound words:**

- compound nouns:

  > sister-in-law; vice-consul

- compound verbs:

  > freeze-dry; dive-bomb

- compound modifiers:

  > a well-considered plan; forward-looking attitudes

  Note that compound modifiers are hyphenated only when they precede the part modified; otherwise, omit the hyphen:

  > The plan was well considered.

  > His attitudes are forward looking.

Also, do not hyphenate a compound modifier that includes an adverb ending in -*ly*:

✓ a well-written novel

✗ a beautifully-written novel

✓ a beautifully written novel

Spell-checking features today will help you determine which compounds to hyphenate, but there is no clear consensus even from one dictionary to another. As always, consistency in your writing style is most important.

3. **Use a hyphen with certain prefixes (all-, self-, ex-) and with prefixes preceding a proper name.** Again, practices vary, so when in doubt consult a dictionary.

> all-star; self-imposed; ex-jockey; pro-Canadian

4. **Use a hyphen to emphasize contrasting prefixes:**

> The coach agreed to give both pre- and post-game interviews.

5. **Use a hyphen to separate written-out compound numbers from one to ninety-nine, and compound fractions:**

> eighty-one years ago; seven-tenths full; two-thirds of a cup

Italics [*italics*]

1. **Use italics for the titles of works published independently, such as books, long poems that are complete books, plays, films, music albums, and long musical compositions:**

> *Fifth Business* is one of my favourite novels.

For articles, essays, short poems, or songs, use quotation marks. If the title itself contains the title of another work, be sure to set it off in the correct style:

- When both titles are books (or book-length poems), you can use quotation marks for the internal one:

> Her latest book is *A Post-Modern Reading of "Hamlet."*

or you can use neither italics nor quotation marks for the title within:

> Her latest book is *A Post-Modern Reading of* Hamlet.

- When the internal title is a book but the main title is not, use italics:

> For more detail, see her recent article, "The Perception of Advertising in McLuhan's *Understanding Media.*"

- When neither title is a book, use single quotation marks:

> Her essay is entitled "Imagery in Keats' 'To Autumn.'"

2. **Use italics to emphasize an idea:**

> It is important that all equipment be washed *immediately*.

Be sparing with this use, interspersing it with other, less intrusive methods of creating emphasis.

3. **Use italics (or quotation marks) to identify a word or phrase that is itself the subject of discussion:**

> The term *peer group* is an example of sociological jargon.

4. **Use italics for foreign words or expressions that have not been naturalized in English:**

> The government was overthrown in a *coup d'état*.
> Her statement was a *cri de coeur*.

Parentheses [( )]

1. **Use parentheses to enclose an explanation, example, or qualification.** Parentheses show that the enclosed material is of incidental importance to the main idea. They make an interruption that is more subtle than one marked off by dashes but more pronounced than one set off by commas:

> My wife (the eldest of five children) is a superb cook and carpenter.

> His latest plan (according to neighbours) is to dam the creek.

Remember that punctuation should not precede parentheses but may follow them if required by the sense of the sentence:

I like coffee in the morning (if it's not instant), but she prefers tea.

If the parenthetical statement comes between two complete sentences, it should be punctuated as a sentence, with the period, question mark, or exclamation mark inside the parentheses:

I finished my essay on April 30. (It was on Aristotle's ethics.) Then I had three weeks to study for the exam.

2. **Use parentheses to enclose references.** See Chapter 7 for details.

Period [.]

1. **Use a period at the end of a sentence.** A period indicates a full stop, not just a pause.

2. **Use a period with some abbreviations.** It is still common, although not mandatory, to use periods in abbreviated titles (Mrs., Dr., Rev., etc.), academic degrees (M.S.W., Ph.D., etc.), and expressions of time (6:30 p.m.).

   However, Canada's adoption of the metric system in 1970 contributed to a trend away from the use of periods in many abbreviations. State and provincial abbreviations do not require periods (BC, NT, PE, NY, DC). In addition, most acronyms for organizations do not use periods (CIDA, CBC, UNESCO, WTO).

3. **Use a period at the end of an indirect question.** Do not use a question mark:

   ✗ He asked if I wanted a substitute?

   ✔ He asked if I wanted a substitute.

   ✗ I wonder where she went?

   ✔ I wonder where she went.

4. **Use a period for questions that are really polite orders:**

   Will you please send him the report by Friday.

Quotation Marks [" "]

1. **Use quotation marks to signify direct discourse (the actual words of a speaker):**

   I asked, "What is the matter?"

   "I have a pain in my big toe," he replied.

2. **Use quotation marks to show that words themselves are the issue:**

   The tennis term "love" comes from the French word for "egg."

   Alternatively, you may italicize the terms in question.

   Sometimes quotation marks are used to mark a slang word or inappropriate usage to show that the writer is aware of the difficulty:

   Several of the "experts" did not seem to know anything about the topic.

   Use this device only when necessary. In general, it's better to let the context show your attitude or to choose another term.

3. **Use quotation marks to enclose the titles of poems, short stories, songs, and articles in books or journals.** In contrast, titles of books, paintings, films, music albums, or long musical compositions are italicized:

   The story I like best in Robert Weaver's *Canadian Short Stories* is "Bernadette" by Mavis Gallant.

4. **Use single quotation marks to enclose quotations within quotations:**

   He said, "Several of the 'experts' did not know anything about the topic."

5. **Do not use quotation marks for indented block quotations (more than four lines).**

Placement of punctuation with quotation marks

- In Canadian usage, a comma or period goes inside the quotation marks:

   He said, "I think we can finish it tonight," but I told him, "Conrad, it's time to go home."

- A semicolon or colon goes outside the quotation marks:

    Conrad calls it "a masterpiece"; I call it junk.

- A question mark, dash, or exclamation mark goes inside quotation marks if it is part of the quotation but outside if it is not:

    She asked, "What *is* that, Conrad?"

    Did she really call it "a piece of junk"?

    You could hardly call it "a masterpiece"!

    I was just telling Louisa, "I think it looks like—" when Conrad walked into the room.

- When a reference is given parenthetically at the end of a quotation, the quotation marks precede the parentheses and the sentence punctuation is at the end:

    Lipsey suggested that we should "abandon the Foreign Investment Review Agency" (Paisley 94).

Semicolon [;]

1. **Use a semicolon to join independent clauses (complete sentences) that are closely related:**

    For five days he worked nonstop; by Saturday he was exhausted.

    His lecture was confusing; no one could understand the terminology.

    A semicolon is especially useful when the second independent clause begins with a conjunctive adverb such as *however, moreover, consequently, nevertheless, in addition,* or *therefore* (usually followed by a comma):

    He ate a whole box of doughnuts; consequently, he felt sick in class.

    It's usually acceptable to follow a semicolon with a coordinating conjunction if the second clause is complicated by other commas:

    Zoltan, my cousin, is a keen jogger in all weather; but sometimes, especially in winter, I think it does him more harm than good.

2. **Use a semicolon to mark the divisions in a complicated series when individual items themselves need commas.** Using a comma to mark the subdivisions and a semicolon to mark the main divisions will help to prevent mix-ups:

✗ He invited Professor Ludvik, the vice-principal, Christine Li, and Dr. Hector Jimenez.

Is the vice-principal Professor Ludvik, Christine Li, or a separate person?

✓ He invited Professor Ludvik; the vice-principal, Christine Li; and Dr. Hector Jimenez.

In a case such as this, the elements separated by the semicolon need not be independent clauses.

Misused Words and Phrases

> **In this chapter, we will examine**
> - words and idioms that are frequently used incorrectly;
> - comparisons of correct and incorrect usage; and
> - examples of problem words and phrases used in context.

accept, except. **Accept** is a verb meaning to *receive affirmatively*; **except**, when used as a verb, means to *exclude*:

> I <u>accept</u> your offer.

> The teacher <u>excepted</u> him from the general punishment.

accompanied by, accompanied with. Use **accompanied by** for people; use **accompanied with** for objects:

> He was <u>accompanied by</u> his wife.

> The brochure arrived, <u>accompanied with</u> a discount coupon.

advice, advise. **Advice** is a noun, **advise** a verb:

> He was <u>advised</u> to ignore the <u>advice</u> of others.

affect, effect. **Affect** is a verb meaning to *influence*; however, it also has a specialized meaning in psychology, referring to a person's emotional state. **Effect** can be either a noun meaning *result* or a verb meaning to *bring about*:

> The eye drops <u>affect</u> his vision.

> Because he was so depressed, he showed no <u>affect</u> when he heard the joke.

The <u>effect</u> of higher government spending is higher inflation.

Negative <u>affect</u> is revealed through frowning.

all ready, already. To be **all ready** is simply to be ready for something; **already** means *beforehand* or *earlier*:

The students were <u>all ready</u> for the lecture to begin.

The professor had <u>already</u> left her office by the time Blair arrived.

all right. Write as two separate words: *all right*. This can mean *safe and sound, in good condition, okay; correct; satisfactory*; or *I agree*:

Are you <u>all right</u>?

The student's answers were <u>all right</u>.

(Note the ambiguity of the second example: does it mean that the answers were all correct or simply satisfactory? In this case, it might be better to use a clearer word.)

all together, altogether. **All together** means *in a group*; **altogether** is an adverb meaning *entirely*:

He was <u>altogether</u> certain that the children were <u>all together</u>.

allusion, illusion. An **allusion** is an indirect reference to something; an **illusion** is a false perception:

The rock image is an <u>allusion</u> to the myth of Sisyphus.

He thought he saw a sea monster, but it was an <u>illusion</u>.

a lot. Write as two separate words: *a lot*.

alternate, alternative. **Alternate** means *every other* or *every second* thing in a series; **alternative** refers to a *choice* between options:

The two sections of the class attended discussion groups on <u>alternate</u> days.

The students could do an extra paper as an <u>alternative</u> to writing the exam.

among, between. Use **among** for three or more persons or objects, **between** for two:

<u>Between</u> you and me, there's trouble <u>among</u> the team members.

amount, number. **Amount** indicates quantity when units are not discrete and not absolute; **number** indicates quantity when units are discrete and absolute:

A large <u>amount</u> of timber.

A large <u>number</u> of students.

See also **less, fewer**.

analysis. The plural is **analyses**.

anyone, any one. **Anyone** is written as two words to give numerical emphasis; otherwise it is written as one word:

<u>Any one</u> of us could do that.

<u>Anyone</u> could do that.

anyways. Non-standard. Use *anyway*.

as, because. **As** is a weaker conjunction than **because** and may be confused with *when*:

✗ <u>As</u> I was working, I ate at my desk.

✓ <u>Because</u> I was working, I ate at my desk.

as to. A common feature of bureaucratese. Replace it with a single-word preposition such as *about* or *on*:

✗ They were concerned <u>as to</u> the range of disagreement.

✓ They were concerned <u>about</u> the range of disagreement.

✗   They recorded his comments <u>as to</u> the treaty.

✓   They recorded his comments <u>on</u> the treaty.

bad, badly. **Bad** is an adjective meaning *not good*:

> The meat tastes <u>bad</u>.
>
> He felt <u>bad</u> about forgetting the dinner party.

Badly is an adverb meaning *not well*; when used with the verbs **want** or **need**, it means *very much*:

> She thought he played the villain's part <u>badly</u>.
>
> I <u>badly</u> need a new suit.

beside, besides. **Beside** is a preposition meaning *next to*:

> She worked <u>beside</u> her assistant.

Besides has two uses: as a preposition it means *in addition to*; as a conjunctive adverb it means *moreover*:

> <u>Besides</u> recommending the changes, the consultants are implementing them.
>
> It was time for lunch; <u>besides</u>, it was hot and we wanted to rest.

between. See **among**.

bring, take. One **brings** something to a closer place and **takes** it to a farther one:

> <u>Take</u> it with you when you go.
>
> Next time you come to visit, <u>bring</u> your friend along.

can, may. **Can** means to *be able*; **may** means to *have permission*:

> <u>Can</u> you fix the lock?
>
> <u>May</u> I have another piece of cake?

In speech, **can** is used to cover both meanings; in formal writing, however, you should observe the distinction.

can't hardly. A faulty combination of the phrases **can't** and **can hardly**. Use one or the other:

> He <u>can't</u> swim.
>
> He <u>can hardly</u> swim.

cite, sight, site. To **cite** something is to *quote* or *mention* it as an example or authority; **sight** can be used in many ways, all of which relate to the ability to *see*; **site** refers to a specific *location*, a particular place at which something is located:

> You need to <u>cite</u> that source in your essay.
>
> His <u>sight</u> was extremely limited.
>
> That <u>site</u> is perfect for a neighbourhood pub.

complement, compliment. The verb to **complement** means to *complete* or *enhance*; to **compliment** means to *praise*:

> Her ability to analyze data <u>complements</u> her excellent research skills.
>
> I <u>complimented</u> her on her outstanding report.

The same rule applies when these words are used as adjectives. The adjective **complimentary** can also mean *free*:

> Use <u>complementary</u> colours for that design.
>
> That was a <u>complimentary</u> comment.
>
> These are <u>complimentary</u> tickets.

compose, comprise. Both words mean to *constitute* or *make up*, but **compose** is preferred. **Comprise** is correctly used to mean *include, consist of*, or *be composed of*. Using **comprise** in the passive ("is comprised of")—as you might be tempted to do in the second example below—is usually frowned on in formal writing:

> These students will <u>compose</u> the group which will go overseas.
>
> Each paragraph <u>comprises</u> an introduction, an argument, and a conclusion.

continual, continuous. Continual means *repeated over a period of time*; **continuous** means *constant* or *without interruption*:

> The strikes caused <u>continual</u> delays in building the road.
>
> Five days of <u>continuous</u> rain ruined our holiday.

could of. This construction is incorrect, as are **might of, should of,** and **would of.** Replace *of* with *have*:

> ✗   He <u>could of</u> done it.
>
> ✓   He <u>could have</u> done it.
>
> ✓   They <u>might have</u> been there.
>
> ✓   I <u>should have</u> known.
>
> ✓   We <u>would have</u> left earlier.

council, counsel. Council is a noun meaning an *advisory* or *deliberative assembly*. **Counsel** as a noun means *advice* or *lawyer*; as a verb it means to *give advice*.

> The college <u>council</u> meets on Tuesday.
>
> We respect her <u>counsel</u>, since she's seldom wrong.
>
> As a camp counsellor, you may need to <u>counsel</u> parents as well as children.

criterion, criteria. A *criterion* is a standard for judging something. **Criteria** is the plural of **criterion** and thus requires a plural verb:

> These are my <u>criteria</u> for grading the reports.
>
> The major <u>criterion</u> was excellence of design.

data. The plural of **datum**. The set of information, usually in numerical form, that is used for analysis as the basis for a study. Since **data** often refers to a single mass entity, many writers now accept its use with a singular verb and pronoun:

> These data were gathered in an unsystematic fashion.
>
> When the data is in we'll have a look at it.

deduce, deduct. To **deduce** something is to *work it out by reasoning*; to **deduct** means to *subtract* or *take away* from something. The noun form of both words is **deduction**.

> You could deduce from his statement that the plant was about to close.
>
> We will deduct income tax from your January pay.

defence, defense. Both spellings are correct: **defence** is standard in Britain and is somewhat more common in Canada; **defense** is standard in the United States.

delusion, illusion. A **delusion** is a belief or perception that is distorted; an **illusion** is a false belief:

> A common delusion among small business owners is the belief that they will experience a profit in the first year.
>
> The desert pool he thought he saw was an illusion.

dependent, dependant. **Dependent** is an adjective meaning *contingent on* or *subject to*; **dependant** is a noun.

> Suriya's graduation is dependent upon her passing algebra.
>
> She has four dependants.

device, devise. The word ending in **-ice** is the noun; the word ending in **-ise** is the verb.

different than, different from. Use **different from** to compare two persons or things; use **different than** with a full clause:

> You are <u>different from</u> me.
>
> This city is <u>different than</u> it used to be.

diminish, minimize. To **diminish** means to *make* or *become smaller*; to **minimize** means to *reduce* something to the smallest possible amount or size.

> His resolve to travel will <u>diminish</u> as he gets older.
>
> The regulation will <u>minimize</u> the impact of higher prices.

disinterested, uninterested. **Disinterested** implies impartiality or neutrality; **uninterested** implies a lack of interest:

> As a <u>disinterested</u> observer, he was in a good position to judge the issue fairly.
>
> <u>Uninterested</u> in the proceedings, he yawned repeatedly.

due to. Although increasingly used to mean *because of*, **due** is an adjective and therefore needs to modify something:

> ✗   <u>Due to</u> his impatience, we lost the contract. [*Due* is dangling.]
>
> ✓   The loss was <u>due to</u> his impatience.

e.g., i.e. **E.g.** means *for example*; **i.e.** means *that is*. It is incorrect to use them interchangeably.

entomology, etymology. **Entomology** is the study of insects; **etymology** is the study of the derivation and history of words.

exceptional, exceptionable. **Exceptional** means *unusual* or *outstanding*, whereas **exceptionable** means *open to objection* and is generally used in negative contexts:

> His accomplishments are <u>exceptional</u>.

He was ejected from the game because of his <u>exceptionable</u> behaviour.

farther, further. Farther refers to distance, **further** to extent:

He paddled <u>farther</u> than his friends did.

She explained the plan <u>further</u>.

focus. The plural of the noun may be either **focuses** (also spelled **focusses**) or **foci.**

good, well. Good is an adjective that modifies a noun; **well** is an adverb that modifies a verb.

He is a <u>good</u> rugby player.

The experiment went <u>well</u>.

hanged, hung. Hanged means *executed by hanging*. **Hung** means *suspended* or *clung to*:

He was <u>hanged</u> at dawn for the murder.

He <u>hung</u> the picture.

She <u>hung</u> on to the boat when it capsized.

hereditary, heredity. Heredity is a noun; **hereditary** is an adjective. **Heredity** is the biological process whereby characteristics are passed from one generation to the next; **hereditary** describes those characteristics:

<u>Heredity</u> is a factor in the incidence of this disease.

Your asthma may be <u>hereditary</u>.

hopefully. Use **hopefully** as an adverb meaning *full of hope*:

She scanned the horizon <u>hopefully</u>, looking for signs of the missing boat.

In formal writing, using **hopefully** to mean *I hope* is still frowned upon, although it is increasingly common; it's better to use *I hope*:

✗ Hopefully the experiment will go off without a hitch.

✓ I hope the experiment will go off without a hitch.

i.e. Stands for "that is." **I.e.** is not the same as **e.g.** See **e.g.**

illusion. See **delusion.**

incite, insight. Incite is a verb meaning to *stir up*; **insight** is a noun meaning (often sudden) *understanding*.

His intention was to incite an uprising.

Her insight into the situation was remarkable.

infer, imply. To **infer** means to *deduce* or *conclude by reasoning*. It is often confused with **imply**, which means to *suggest* or *insinuate*.

We can infer from the large population density that there is a high demand for services.

The large population density implies that there is a high demand for services.

inflammable, flammable, non-flammable. Despite its **in-** prefix, **inflammable** is not the opposite of **flammable**: both words describe things that are *easily set on fire*. The opposite of **flammable** is **non-flammable**. To prevent any possibility of confusion, it's best to avoid **inflammable** altogether.

irregardless. Non-standard. Use *regardless*.

its, it's. Its is a form of possessive pronoun; **it's** is a contraction of *it is*. Many people mistakenly put an apostrophe in **its** in order to show possession.

✗ The cub wanted it's mother.

✓ The cub wanted its mother.

✓ It's time to leave.

less, fewer. Less is used when units are *not* discrete and *not* absolute (as in "less information"). **Fewer** is used when the units *are* discrete and absolute (as in "fewer details").

lie, lay. To **lie** means to *assume a horizontal position*; to **lay** means to *put down*. The changes of tense often cause confusion:

Present	Past	Past participle	Present participle
lie	lay	lain	lying
lay	laid	laid	laying

✗ I was <u>laying</u> on the couch when he came in.

✓ I was <u>lying</u> on the couch when he came in.

✓ I <u>laid</u> the table for dinner.

✓ She needed to <u>lie</u> down for a minute.

✓ The crew was <u>laying</u> the carpet.

like, as. Like is a preposition, but it is often wrongly used as a conjunction. To join two independent clauses, use the conjunction **as**:

✗ I want to progress <u>like</u> you have this year.

✓ I want to progress <u>as</u> you have this year.

✓ Prof. Dimitriou is <u>like</u> my old school principal.

might of. Incorrect. See **could of.**

minimize. See **diminish.**

mitigate, militate. To **mitigate** means to *reduce the severity* of something; to **militate** against something means to *oppose* it:

This income will <u>mitigate</u> my overdraft problems.

His credentials will <u>militate</u> against the resistance to his appointment.

myself, me. Myself is an intensifier of, not a substitute for, *I* or *me*:

✗ He gave it to John and <u>myself</u>.

✓ He gave it to John and <u>me</u>.

✗   Jane and <u>myself</u> are invited.

✓   Jane and <u>I</u> are invited.

✓   I hesitate to mention <u>myself</u> here.

nor, or. Use **nor** with **neither**; use **or** by itself or with **either**:

He is <u>neither</u> overworked <u>nor</u> underfed.

The plant is <u>either</u> diseased <u>or</u> dried out.

off of. Remove the unnecessary **of**:

✗   The fence kept the children <u>off of</u> the premises.

✓   The fence kept the children <u>off</u> the premises.

phenomenon. A singular noun: the plural is **phenomena.**

plaintiff, plaintive. A **plaintiff** is a person who brings a case against someone else in court; **plaintive** is an adjective meaning *sorrowful.*

populace, populous. Populace is a noun meaning the *people* of a place; **populous** is an adjective meaning *thickly inhabited*:

The <u>populace</u> of Hilltop village is not well educated.

With so many people in such a small area, Hilltop village is a <u>populous</u> place.

practice, practise. Both of these spellings have become acceptable for either the noun or the verb. Just be consistent in whatever form you choose.

precede, proceed. To **precede** is to *go before* (earlier) or *in front of* others; to **proceed** is to *go on* or *ahead*:

The faculty will <u>precede</u> the students into the hall.

The medal winners will <u>proceed</u> to the front of the hall.

prescribe, **proscribe**. These words are sometimes confused, although they have quite different meanings. **Prescribe** means to *advise the use of* or *impose authoritatively*. **Proscribe** means to *reject, denounce*, or *ban*:

> The professor <u>prescribed</u> the conditions under which the equipment could be used.

> The student government <u>proscribed</u> the publication of unsigned editorials in the newspaper.

principle, **principal**. **Principle** is a noun meaning a *general truth* or *law*; **principal** can be used as either a noun, referring to the *head of a school* or a *capital sum of money*, or an adjective, meaning *chief*:

> Bev Dawson is the <u>principal</u> of Richmond Secondary School.

> The <u>principal</u> reason for refusing is our lack of funds.

> His lack of <u>principle</u> is a major problem.

rational, **rationale**. **Rational** is an adjective meaning *logical* or *able to reason*. **Rationale** is a noun meaning *explanation*:

> That was not a <u>rational</u> decision.

> The president sent around a memo explaining the <u>rationale</u> for her decision.

real, **really**. **Real**, an adjective, means *true* or *genuine*; **really**, an adverb, means *actually, truly, very*, or *extremely*:

> The nugget was <u>real</u> gold.

> The nugget was <u>really</u> valuable.

seasonable, **seasonal**. **Seasonable** means *usual* or *suitable for the season*; **seasonal** means *of, depending on*, or *varying with the season*:

> It's quite cool today, but we can expect the return of <u>seasonable</u> temperatures later this week.

You must consider <u>seasonal</u> temperature changes when you pack for such a long trip.

should of. Incorrect. See **could of.**

their, there. Their is the possessive form of the third person plural pronoun. **There** is usually an adverb, meaning *at that place* or *at that point*:

They parked <u>their</u> bikes against the fence.

I'll meet you <u>there</u> at midnight.

tortuous, torturous. The adjective **tortuous** means *full of twists and turns* or *circuitous.* **Torturous,** derived from *torture*, means *involving torture* or *excruciating*:

To avoid heavy traffic, they took a <u>tortuous</u> route home.

The concert was a <u>torturous</u> experience for the audience.

translucent, transparent. A **translucent** substance permits light to pass through, but not enough for a person to see through it; a **transparent** substance permits light to pass unobstructed, so that objects can be seen clearly through it.

turbid, turgid. Turbid, with respect to a liquid or colour, means *muddy, not clear,* or (with respect to literary style) *confused.* **Turgid** means *swollen, inflated,* or *enlarged,* or (again with reference to literary style) *pompous* or *bombastic.*

unique. This word, which means *of which there is only one* or *unequalled,* is both overused and misused. Since there are no degrees of comparison—one thing cannot be "more unique" than another—expressions such as *very unique* or *quite unique* are incorrect.

while. To avoid misreading, use **while** only when you mean *at the same time that.* Do not use **while** as a substitute for *although, whereas,* or *but*:

✗ <u>While</u> she's getting fair marks, she'd like to do better.

✗   I headed for home, <u>while</u> she decided to stay.

✓   He fell asleep <u>while</u> he was reading.

-wise. Never use **-wise** as a suffix to form new words when you mean *with regard to*:

✗   <u>Sales-wise</u>, the company did better last year.

✓   The company's sales increased last year.

your, you're. Your is a possessive adjective; **you're** is a contraction of *you are*:

Be sure to take <u>your</u> passport with you.

<u>You're</u> likely to miss <u>your</u> train.

Glossary

abstract. A summary accompanying a formal scientific report or paper, briefly outlining the contents.

abstract language. Language that deals with theoretical, intangible concepts or details: e.g., *justice, goodness, truth*. (Compare **concrete language**.)

acronym. A pronounceable word made up of the first letters of the words in a phrase or name: e.g., *NATO* (from *North Atlantic Treaty Organization*). A group of initial letters that are pronounced separately is an **initialism**: e.g., *CBC, NHL*.

active voice. See **voice**.

adjectival phrase (or **adjectival clause**). A group of words modifying a noun or pronoun: e.g., *the dog that belongs to my brother*.

adjective. A word that modifies or describes a noun or pronoun: e.g., *red, beautiful, solemn*.

adverb. A word that modifies or qualifies a verb, adjective, or adverb, often answering a question such as *how? why? when?* or *where?*: e.g., *slowly, fortunately, early, abroad*. (See also **conjunctive adverb**.)

adverbial phrase (or **adverbial clause**). A group of words modifying a verb, adjective, or adverb: e.g., *The dog ran with great speed*.

agreement. Consistency in tense, number, or person between related parts of a sentence: e.g., between subject and verb, or noun and related pronoun.

ambiguity. Vague or equivocal language; meaning that can be taken two ways.

antecedent (or **referent**). The noun for which a following pronoun stands: e.g., *cats* in *Cats are happiest when they are sleeping*.

appositive. A word or phrase that identifies a preceding noun or pronoun: e.g., *Mrs. Jones, my aunt, is sick*. The second phrase is said to be **in apposition to** the first.

article. See **definite article, indefinite article**.

assertion. A positive statement or claim: e.g., *The data are inconclusive*.

auxiliary verb. A verb used to form the tenses, moods, and voices of other verbs: e.g., *am* in *I am swimming*. The main auxiliary verbs in English are *be, do, have, can, could, may, might, must, shall, should*, and *will*.

bibliography. 1. A list of works used or referred to in writing an essay or report. 2. A reference book listing works available on a particular subject.

case. Any of the inflected forms of a pronoun (see **inflection**).

> **Subjective case**. *I, we, you, he, she, it, they*
>
> **Objective case**. *me, us, you, him, her, it, them*
>
> **Possessive case**. *my/mine, your/yours, our/ours, his, her/hers, its, their/theirs*

circumlocution. A roundabout or circuitous expression, often used in a deliberate attempt to be vague or evasive: e.g., *in a family way* for "pregnant"; *at this point in time* for "now."

clause. A group of words containing a subject and predicate. An **independent clause** can stand by itself as a complete sentence: e.g., *I bought a hamburger.* A **subordinate** (or **dependent**) **clause** cannot stand by itself but must be connected to another clause: e.g., *Because I was hungry, I bought a hamburger.*

cliché. A phrase or idea that has lost its impact through overuse and betrays a lack of original thought: e.g., *slept like a log, gave 110 per cent.*

collective noun. A noun that is singular in form but refers to a group: e.g., *family, team, jury.* It may take either a singular or plural verb, depending on whether it refers to individual members or to the group as a whole.

comma splice. See **run-on sentence.**

complement. A completing word or phrase that usually follows a linking verb to form a **subjective complement**: e.g., (1) *He is my father;* (2) *That cigar smells terrible.* If the complement is an adjective it is sometimes called a **predicate adjective.** An **objective complement** completes the direct object rather than the subject: e.g., *We found him honest and trustworthy.*

complex sentence. A sentence containing a dependent clause as well as an independent one: e.g., *I bought the ring, although it was expensive.*

compound sentence. A sentence containing two or more independent clauses: e.g., *I saw the accident and I reported it.* A sentence is called **compound-complex** if it contains a dependent clause as well as two independent ones: e.g., *When the fog lifted, I saw the accident and I reported it.*

conclusion. The part of an essay in which the findings are pulled together or the implications revealed so that the reader has a sense of closure or completion.

concrete language. Specific language that communicates particular details: e.g., *red corduroy dress, three long-stemmed roses.* (Compare **abstract language.**)

conjunction. An uninflected word used to link words, phrases, or clauses. A **coordinating conjunction** (e.g., *and, or, but, for, yet*) links two equal parts of a sentence. A **subordinating conjunction**, placed at the beginning of a subordinate clause, shows the logical dependence of that clause on another: e.g., (1) *Although I am poor, I am happy;* (2) *While others slept, he studied.* **Correlative conjunctions** are pairs of coordinating conjunctions (see **correlatives**).

conjunctive adverb. A type of adverb that shows the logical relation between the phrase or clause that it modifies and a preceding one: e.g., (1) *I sent the letter; it never arrived, however.* (2) *The battery died; therefore, the car wouldn't start.*

connotation. The range of ideas or meanings suggested by a certain word in addition to its literal meaning. Apparent synonyms, such as *poor* and *underprivileged*, may have different connotations. (Compare **denotation.**)

context. The text surrounding a particular passage that helps to establish its meaning.

contraction. A word formed by combining and shortening two words: e.g., *isn't* from "is not"; *we're* from "we are."

coordinate construction. A grammatical construction that uses correlatives.

copula verb. See **linking verb.**

correlatives (or **coordinates**). Pairs of correlative conjunctions: e.g., *either/or; neither/nor; not only/but (also).*

dangling modifier. A modifying word or phrase (often including a participle) that is not grammatically connected to any part of the sentence: e.g., *Walking to school, the street was slippery.*

definite article. The word *the*, which precedes a noun and implies that it has already been mentioned or is common knowledge. (Compare **indefinite article.**)

demonstrative pronoun. A pronoun that points out something: e.g., (1) *This is his reason*; (2) *That looks like my lost earring*. When used to modify a noun or pronoun, a demonstrative pronoun becomes a **demonstrative adjective**: e.g., *this hat*, *those* people.

denotation. The literal or dictionary meaning of a word. (Compare **connotation.**)

dependent clause. See **clause**.

diction. The choice of words with regard to their tone, degree of formality, or register. Formal diction is the language of orations and serious essays. The informal diction of everyday speech or conversational writing can, at its extreme, become slang.

direct object. See **object**.

discourse. Talk, either oral or written. **Direct discourse** (or **direct speech**) gives the actual words spoken or written: e.g., *Donne said, "No man is an island."* In writing, direct discourse is put in quotation marks. **Indirect discourse** (or **indirect speech**) gives the meaning of the speech rather than the actual words. In writing, indirect discourse is not put in quotation marks: e.g., *He said that no one exists in an island of isolation.*

ellipsis. Three spaced periods indicating an omission from a quoted passage. At the end of a sentence use four periods.

essay. A literary composition on any subject. Some essays are descriptive or narrative, but in an academic setting most are expository (explanatory) or argumentative.

euphemism. A word or phrase used to avoid some other word or phrase that might be considered offensive or blunt: e.g., *pass away* for *die*.

expletive. 1. A word or phrase used to fill out a sentence without adding to the sense: e.g., *To be sure, it's not an ideal situation*. 2. A swear word.

exploratory writing. The informal writing done to help generate ideas before formal planning begins.

fused sentence. See **run-on sentence**.

general language. Language that lacks specific details; abstract language.

gerund. A verbal (part-verb) that functions as a noun and is marked by an *-ing* ending: e.g., *Swimming can help you become fit.*

grammar. The study of the forms and relations of words and of the rules governing their use in speech and writing.

hypothesis. A supposition or trial proposition made as a starting point for further investigation.

hypothetical instance. A supposed occurrence, often indicated by a clause beginning with *if*.

indefinite article. The word *a* or *an*, which introduces a noun and suggests that it is non-specific. (Compare **definite article.**)

independent clause. See **clause**.

indirect discourse (or **indirect speech**). See **discourse**.

indirect object. See **object**.

infinitive. A type of verbal not connected to any subject: e.g., *to ask*. The **base infinitive** omits the *to*: e.g., *ask*.

inflection. The change in the form of a word to indicate number, person, case, tense, or degree.

initialism. See **acronym**.

intensifier (or **qualifier**). A word that modifies and adds emphasis to another word or phrase: e.g., *very tired, quite happy, I myself.*

interjection. An abrupt remark or exclamation, usually accompanied by an exclamation mark: e.g., *Oh dear! Alas!*

interrogative sentence. A sentence that asks a question: e.g., *What is the time?*

intransitive verb. A verb that does not take a direct object: e.g., *fall, sleep, talk.* (Compare **transitive verb**.)

introduction. A section at the beginning of an essay that tells the reader what is going to be discussed and why.

italics. Slanting type used for emphasis or to indicate the title of a book or journal.

jargon. Technical terms used unnecessarily or in inappropriate places: e.g., *peer-group interaction* for "friendship."

linking verb (or **copula verb**). A verb such as *be*, *seem*, or *feel*, used to join subject to complement: e.g., *The apples were ripe.*

literal meaning. The primary, or denotative, meaning of a word.

logical indicator. A word or phrase—usually a conjunction or conjunctive adverb—that shows the logical relation between sentences or clauses: e.g., *since, furthermore, therefore.*

misplaced modifier. A word or group of words that can cause confusion because it is not placed next to the element it should modify: e.g., *I only ate the pie.* [Revised: *I ate only the pie.*]

modifier. A word or group of words that describes or limits another element in the sentence: e.g., *The woman with the black hat donated a million dollars.*

mood 1. As a grammatical term, the form that shows a verb's function.

  Indicative mood. *She is going.*

  Imperative mood. *Go!*

  Interrogative mood. *Is she going?*

  Subjunctive mood. *It is important that she go.*

2. When applied to literature generally, the atmosphere or tone created by the author.

non-restrictive modifier (or **non-restrictive element**). See **restrictive modifier**.

noun. An inflected part of speech marking a person, place, thing, idea, action, or feeling, and usually serving as subject, object, or complement. A **common noun** is a general term: e.g., *dog, paper, automobile.* A **proper noun** is a specific name: e.g., *Martin, Sudbury.*

object. 1. A noun or pronoun that completes the action of a verb is called a **direct object**: e.g., *He passed the puck.* An **indirect object** is the person or thing receiving the direct object: e.g., *He passed Marcus* (indirect object) *the puck* (direct object). 2. The noun or pronoun in a group of words beginning with a preposition: e.g., *at the house, about her, for me.*

objective complement. See **complement**.

objectivity. A position or stance taken without personal bias or prejudice. (Compare **subjectivity**.)

outline. With regard to an essay or report, a brief sketch of the main parts; a written plan.

paragraph. A unit of sentences arranged logically to explain or describe an idea, event, or object. The start of a paragraph is sometimes marked by indentation of the first line.

parallel wording. Wording in which a series of items has a similar grammatical form: e.g., *At her wedding my grandmother promised to love, to honour, and to obey her husband.*

paraphrase. Restate in different words.

parentheses. Curved lines enclosing and setting off a passage; not to be confused with square brackets.

parenthetical element. A word or phrase inserted as an explanation or afterthought into a passage that is grammatically complete without it: e.g., *My musical career, if it can be called that, consisted of playing the triangle in kindergarten.*

participle. A verbal (part-verb) that functions as an adjective. Participles can be either **present**: (e.g., *speaking to the assembly*) or **past** (e.g., *spoken before the jury*).

part of speech. Each of the major categories into which words are placed according to their grammatical function. Traditional grammar classifies words based on eight parts of speech: verbs, nouns, pronouns, adjectives, adverbs, prepositions, conjunctions, and interjections.

passive voice. See **voice**.

past participle. See **participle**.

periodic sentence. A sentence in which the normal order is inverted or in which an essential element is suspended until the very end: e.g., *Out of the house, past the grocery store, through the school yard, and down the railway tracks raced the frightened boy.*

person. In grammar, the three classes of personal pronouns referring to the person speaking (**first person**), the person spoken to (**second person**), and the person spoken about

(**third person**). With verbs, only the third-person singular has a distinctive inflected form.

personal pronoun. See **pronoun**.

phrase. A unit of words lacking a subject-predicate combination, typically forming part of a clause. The most common kind is the **prepositional phrase**—a unit consisting of a preposition and an object: e.g., *They are waiting at the house.*

plural. Indicating two or more in number. Nouns, pronouns, and verbs all have plural forms.

possessive case. See **case**.

prefix. An element placed in front of the root form of a word to make a new word: e.g., *pro-, in-, sub-, anti-*. (Compare **suffix**.)

preposition. The introductory word in a unit of words containing an object, thus forming a prepositional phrase: e.g., *under the tree, before my time.*

pronoun. A word that stands in for a noun: e.g., *she, this.*

punctuation. A conventional system of signs (e.g., comma, period, semicolon) used to indicate stops or divisions in a sentence and to make meaning clearer.

reference works. Sources consulted when preparing an essay or report.

referent. See **antecedent**.

reflexive verb. A verb that has an identical subject and object: e.g., *Isabel taught herself to skate.*

register. The degree of formality in word choice and sentence structure.

relative clause. A clause introduced by a relative pronoun: e.g., *The man who came to dinner is my uncle.*

relative pronoun. *Who, which, what, that*, or their compounds, used to introduce an adjective or noun clause: e.g., *the house that Jack built*; *whatever you say*.

restrictive modifier (or **restrictive element**). A phrase or clause that identifies or is essential to the meaning of a term: e.g., *The book that my aunt gave me is missing*. It should not be set off by commas. A **non-restrictive modifier** is not needed to identify the term and is usually set off by commas: e.g., *This book, which my aunt gave me, is one of my favourites*.

rhetorical question. A question asked and answered by a writer or speaker to draw attention to a point; no response is expected on the part of the audience: e.g., *How significant are these findings? In my opinion, they are extremely significant, for the following reasons. . . .*

run-on sentence. A sentence that goes on beyond the point where it should have stopped. The term covers both the **comma splice** (two sentences incorrectly joined by a comma) and the **fused sentence** (two sentences incorrectly joined without any punctuation).

sentence. A grammatical unit that includes both a subject and a verb. The end of a sentence is marked by a period.

sentence fragment. A group of words lacking either a subject or a verb; an incomplete sentence.

simple sentence. A sentence made up of only one clause: e.g., *Joaquim climbed the tree*.

slang. Colloquial speech considered inappropriate for academic writing; it is often used in a special sense by a particular group: e.g., *dope* for "good" or *diss* for "disrespect."

split infinitive. A construction in which a word is placed between *to* and the base verb: e.g., *to completely finish*. Many still object to this kind of construction, but splitting infinitives is sometimes necessary when the alternatives are awkward or ambiguous.

squinting modifier. A kind of misplaced modifier that could be connected to elements on either side, making meaning ambiguous: e.g., *When he wrote the letter finally his boss thanked him*.

standard English. The English currently spoken or written by literate people and widely accepted as the correct and standard form.

subject. In grammar, the noun or noun equivalent with which the verb agrees and about which the rest of the clause is predicated: e.g., *They swim every day when the pool is open*.

subjective complement. See **complement**.

subjectivity. A stance that is based on personal feelings or opinions and is not impartial. (Compare **objectivity**.)

subjunctive. See **mood**.

subordinate clause. See **clause**.

subordinating conjunction. See **conjunction**.

subordination. Making one clause in a sentence dependent on another.

suffix. An element added to the end of a word to form a derivative: e.g., *prepare, preparation*; *sing, singing*. (Compare **prefix**.)

synonym. A word with the same dictionary meaning as another word: e.g., *begin* and *commence*.

syntax. Sentence construction; the grammatical arrangement of words and phrases.

tense. A set of inflected forms taken by a verb to indicate the time (i.e., past, present, future) of the action.

theme. A recurring or dominant idea.

thesis statement. A one-sentence assertion that gives the central argument of an essay.

topic sentence. The sentence in a paragraph that expresses the main or controlling idea.

transition word. A word that shows the logical relation between sentences or parts of a sentence and thus helps to signal the change from one idea to another: e.g., *therefore, also, however.*

transitive verb. A verb that takes an object: e.g., *hit, bring, cover.* (Compare **intransitive verb**.)

usage. The way in which a word or phrase is normally and correctly used; accepted practice.

verb. That part of a predicate expressing an action, state of being, or condition that tells what a subject is or does. Verbs are inflected to show tense (time). The principal parts of a verb are the three basic forms from which all tenses are made: the base infinitive, the past tense, and the past participle.

verbal. A word that is similar in form to a verb but does not function as one: a participle, a gerund, or an infinitive.

voice. The form of a verb that shows whether the subject acted (**active voice**) or was acted upon (**passive voice**): e.g., *He stole the money* (active). *The money was stolen by him* (passive). Only transitive verbs (verbs taking objects) can be passive.

Index

abbreviations, and periods, 179
abstract, in lab report, 46, 47
abstractions, 149
abstract nouns, 52
accept/except, 183
accompanied by/with, 183
accuracy: illustrations, 72; quotations, 74
acknowledgement of sources, 33–5, 73; *see also* documenting sources
active voice, 49, 147–8
ad hominem attack, 27
adjectives: and commas, 171–2; and modifiers, 163; use of, 145
adverbs, 143–4, 145, 151–2
advice/advise, 183
affect/effect, 183–4
all ready/already, 184
all right, 184
all together/altogether, 184
allusion/illusion, 184
a lot, 184
alphanumeric numbering system, 66
alternate/alternative, 184–5
among/between, 185
amount/number, 185
analysis, 185
analytic book report, 42–4
anecdote, in introduction, 29
annotated bibliography, 108–9
anthology, *see* edited book (selection)
anyone/any one, 185
anyways, 185
APA style (American Psychological Association): annotated bibliography, 108; in-text citations, 90–3; quotations and quotation marks, 90; references, 93–7
APA Style Guide to Electronic References, 90, 92, 96
apostrophe, 167–8
appendix, in business report, 63
application: by letter, 134–5; online, 136
appositives, and comma, 172
argumentative essays, 2, 13–14, 19–20
arguments, in essay, 25–7
articles: in APA style, 90–2, 94–5; in Chicago style, 99, 102–3; in CSE style, 107; DOI system, 95; in MLA style, 77–8, 79–80, 84–5, 87–8; *see also* journals; magazines; newspapers

as/because, 185
as to, 185–6
attachments, in lab report, 46, 51
audience, in oral presentation, 111, 115
author-date system, in Chicago style, 101–3, 109
author(s): in APA style, 90–2, 93–4; in Chicago style, 97–8, 101–2; in CSE style, 105–6; in MLA style, 77–8, 79–80, 81–2; *see also* corporate authors

backups, 38
bad/badly, 186
Baker, Sheridan, 27, 30
bar charts, 70–1
because/as, 185
beside/besides, 186
between/among, 185
bias-free language, 5–7
bibliographic details, 18
bibliography, annotated, 108–9
bibliography and notes, in Chicago style, 97–101, 103
block quotations: in APA style, 90; general use, 74; in MLA style, 76–7, 78–9
blogs and blog entry: in APA style, 96–7; in Chicago style, 100; in MLA style, 90; as source of information, 18
book report: definition and types, 39; writing of (*see* writing a book report)
book review, 41–4
books: in APA style, 90–2, 93–4; chapter of, 83–4, 98–9, 102; in Chicago style, 97–9, 101–2; in CSE style, 106–7; in MLA style, 77–8, 79–80, 81–4, 89; selection, 83–4, 94, 107
brackets, 168
bring/take, 186
business reports, *see* planning a business report; writing a business report

calculations, in lab reports, 49
Canadian Oxford Dictionary Online, 138
Canadian usage, 138
can/may, 186–7
can't hardly, 187
cause and effect, in essay, 24
change: for examinations, 120; in three-C approach, 11, 12
chapter of a book: in Chicago style, 98–9, 102; in MLA style, 83–4

charts, use and types, 69–72
Chicago Manual of Style, The (CMS), 97
Chicago style: author-date system, 97, 101–3, 109; notes and bibliography, 97–101, 109
Chicago-Style Citation Quick Guide, 97
circumlocutions, 146–7
citation-name system, in CSE style, 105–8
citations, *see* documenting sources; in-text citations; references
citation-sequence system, in CSE style, 104–5
cite/sight/site, 187
clarity, in style, 137–45
classification, in essay, 23–4
clichés, 146–7
collaboration, 58–9, 117–18
collective nouns, 158
colon, 168–9, 181
comma, 169–74, 180
comma splice, 155, 170
comparisons, 24–5, 61, 166
complement/compliment, 187
components: for examinations, 120; in three-C approach, 11–12
compose/comprise, 187–8
compound modifiers, and hyphens, 176–7
compound subjects, 157–8
compound words, division with hyphens, 176–7
conciseness, 54, 145–7
conclusion: in business report, 60; of essay, 29–31; in lab report, 46, 51
concrete details, 149
conjunctions and conjunctive adverbs, 143–4, 170–1
connotative meaning, 138
context: for examinations, 120; in three-C approach, 11, 12–13
continual/continuous, 187–8
contractions, 4–5, 168
contrast, 151
coordinating conjunctions: and commas, 169–71, 174; and independent clauses, 154–5; and semicolons, 181
corporate authors: in APA style, 91–2, 93–4; in Chicago style, 98, 101; in CSE style, 106; in MLA style, 79–80, 82
correlative construction, 151–2
correlatives, 166
could of, 188
council/counsel, 188
criterion/criteria, 188
CSE style (Council of Science Editors): citation-name system, 105–8; citation-sequence system, 104–5; name-year system, 104
culture, and bias-free language, 7

dangling modifiers, 164–5
dash, 174–5

data, 189
databases, in MLA style, 88
dates, and en dash, 175
decimal numbering system, 66
deduce/deduct, 189
defence/defense, 189
definitions, 23, 65
delusion/illusion, 189
denotative meaning, 138
dependent/dependant, 189
device/devise, 189
diction, and style, 137–41
dictionaries, 137–8
different than/from, 190
diminish/minimize, 190
discussion, in lab report, 46, 50–1
discussion list, in MLA style, 90
discussion of findings, in business report, 60, 61
disinterested/uninterested, 190
documenting sources: annotated bibliography, 108–9; APA style, 90–7; Chicago style, 97–103; CSE style, 104–8; formatting, 75; MLA style, 75–90; overview and purpose, 73; quotations, 73–5; secondary sources, 73; systems and styles, 75
DOI system (digital object identifier): in APA style, 95–6; in Chicago style, 99
domain names, 17
drama, in MLA style, 78–9
due to, 190

each, 157
edited book (selection): in APA style, 94; in CSE style, 107; in MLA style, 83–4
editing stage, 35–7, 41
edition of a book, in MLA style, 83
editor: in APA style, 94; in Chicago style, 98, 102; in CSE style, 107; in MLA style, 83
effect/affect, 183–4
e.g., 190
either, 157
electronic application, 136
electronic databases, 16–17
electronic sources: in APA style, 92–3, 95–6; in MLA style, 80, 86–7; *see also* online sources
ellipsis, 75, 175–6
e-mail: in Chicago style, 101; in MLA style, 89
em dash, 174
en dash, 175
end reference, in CSE style, 104, 105, 106
English usage, 138–9
entomology/etylomogy, 190
equipment, in lab report, 47–8
essay exams, 121–3
essay planning, *see* planning an essay
essay writing, *see* writing an essay

et al., 91

examinations: educated guesses in, 125–6; essay exams, 121–3; objective test, 124–7; open-book exams, 123; preparation, 119–21; review for, 119–20; take-home exams, 124

except/accept, 183

exceptional/exceptionable, 190–1

exclamation mark, 176

experiments, *see* writing a lab report

expository essays, 2, 13–14, 20–1

farther/further, 191

first draft of essay, 22

first-person pronouns, 4

flammable/non-flammable/inflammable, 192

focus, 191

forcefulness, in style, 147–52

foreign words, and italics, 178

formal *vs.* informal tone, 3–5

formatting: business report, 63; documenting sources, 75; of essay, 37–8; results section of lab report, 49; resumé, 128–34; visual aids to oral presentation, 113

four Rs, 55–8

full circle, in conclusion, 31

functional resumé, 130, 133–4

funnel approach, 27–8, 30

future tense, 159

gender, and bias-free language, 6–7

gerund, 163

good/well, 191

government agencies, as author, *see* corporate authors

grammar, common errors, 153–66

grammar checkers, 36–7

graphs, 49–50, 66

group work: oral presentation, 117–18; reports from, 58–9

handout, in oral presentation, 111

handwriting, in exams, 122–3

hanged/hung, 191

he, 6

headings, in business reports, 65

hereditary/heredity, 191

hopefully, 191–2

hyphen, 176–7

hypothesis, in lab report, 45

I: in business reports, 64–5; and *myself,* 193–4; use of, 4, 161–2

i.e., 190, 192

if, and verbs, 159

illusion/delusion, 189

illustrations: appeal of, 66–7; in business reports, 66; charts, 69–72; dangers to avoid, 72; graphs, 49–50, 66; importance and guidelines, 68–9; oral presentations, 112–14, 115–16; organization of materials, 114; tables, 49, 66, 69, 72; visual appeal tips, 66–7

incite/insight, 192

in-class seminar, *see* oral presentation

inclusive numbers or dates, and en dash, 175

independent clauses: and commas, 154–5, 169–71; reduction of, 146; and semicolons, 181–2; in sentences, 153–5

indirect questions, 179

infer/imply, 192

inflammable/flammable/non-flammable, 192

informative book report, 39–41

integrated quotations, in MLA style, 76–7, 79

interruption, and comma, 172

in-text citations: in APA style, 90–3; in CSE style, 104–5; in MLA style, 75, 77–80

introduction: approaches to, 27–9; book reports, 42; in business report, 60; in lab report, 46, 47; purpose, 27

inverse funnel approach, 30

irregardless, 192

it, and pronouns, 161

italics: in MLA style, 75–6, 86; in quotations, 74; use of, 177–8

It is . . . , 147

its/it's, 168, 192

jargon, 140

journals: in APA style, 94, 96; in Chicago style, 99, 102; in CSE style, 107; in MLA style, 84, 87–8; online research, 16–17

lab report writing, *see* writing a lab report

language, bias-free, 5–7

learning disabilities, and examinations, 120–1

lecture: in APA style, 95; in Chicago style, 101, 103; in MLA style, 85

length of essay, 3

less/fewer, 193

letter of application, 134–6

letter of transmittal, 62–3

library resources, in research of topic, 16–17

lie/lay, 193

like/as, 193

line charts, 70

linking words, 143–4

lists, 66, 166, 169

literary review, 44

literary works: in MLA style, 78–9; and verb tenses, 159–60

a lot, 184

-ly, hyphenation, 177

magazines: in APA style, 95; in Chicago style, 99, 103; in CSE style, 107; in MLA style, 84, 88
materials section, in lab report, 46, 47–8
may/can, 186–7
me: and *myself,* 193–4; and pronouns, 162–3
method section, in lab report, 46, 47–9
Microsoft Office, charts, 69–71
might of, 193
minimize/diminish, 190
mitigate/militate, 193
MLA Handbook, 75
MLA style (Modern Language Association): annotated bibliography, 108; in-text citations, 75, 77–80; overview and formatting, 75–6; quotations in, 76–7; works cited, 75, 81–90
modifiers: and comma, 172–3; compound, 176–7; use of, 163–5
multiple-choice tests, 124–7
myself/me, 193–4

name-year system, in CSE style, 104
neither, 157
new angle, in conclusion, 30–1
newspapers: in APA style, 94–5, 96; in Chicago style, 99, 103; in CSE style, 107; in MLA style, 85, 88
non-flammable/inflammable/flammable, 192
non-periodical publication, in MLA style, 89
nor/or, 194
notes and bibliography, Chicago style, 97–101, 103
note taking, 18–19, 40
noun clusters, 145–6
noun phrases, 156
nouns: collective, 158; in lab report, 52; and pronouns, 160–1
number/amount, 185
numbering, in business reports, 63, 65–6
numbers, punctuation, 175, 176, 177

objective pronouns, 162–3
objective test, 124–7
objectivity, in business reports, 55, 64–5
off of, 194
omissions, and ellipsis, 175
one, and pronouns, 161–2
online application, 136
online catalogues, in libraries, 16
online dictionary, in APA style, 96
online encyclopedia, in APA style, 96
online publications, in MLA style, 88–9
online sources: acknowledgement, 35; in Chicago style, 102; in CSE style, 107–8; finding and evaluating, 16–18; in MLA style, 86–8, 89; notes and bibliography, 99; references, 96; *see also* electronic sources; websites

open-book exams, 123
oral presentation: group presentations, 110, 117–18; preparation, 110–14; talk delivery, 114–17; visual aids, 112–14, 115–16
organization of business report, 55, 59–61
organization of essay, 22–7, 36–7; *see also* planning an essay
organizations, as author, *see* corporate authors
or/nor, 194
outline: examples, 19–21; guidelines, 21–2; in oral presentation, 111; in planning an essay, 19–22
Oxford comma, 171

pairs, usage, 165
paper(s): in Chicago style, 101, 103; in CSE style, 107
paragraphs, and style, 141–5
parallel phrasing, 166
parentheses, 178–9
parenthetical element, and comma, 172
passive constructions and voice: avoidance of, 147–8; in business reports, 64; with "he" or "she," 6; in lab report, 49, 52–3
past perfect tense, 158–9
past tense, in lab report, 49
period, 179, 180
periodic sentences, 150–1
personal pronouns, in business reports, 64–5
personal subjects, 148–9
persuasive essays, 2, 13–14, 19–20
phenomenon, 194
pie charts, 71
plagiarism, 32–5, 73
plain English, 138–9
plaintiff/plaintive, 194
planning a business report: beginnings, 62–3; as a collaboration, 58–9; endings, 63; four Rs, 55–8; organization of information and details, 59–61
planning an essay: importance, 8–9; note taking, 18–19; outline creation, 19–22; prescribed topic, 13; primary material, 9–10; subject analysis, 10–13; thesis development, 13–16; topic research, 16–18
poetry, in MLA style, 78–9
polite orders, 179
populace/populous, 194
possession, and apostrophe, 167–8
possessive pronouns, 168
practice/practise, 194
precede/proceed, 194
preciseness, 65, 140
precise thesis, 15–16
prefixes, hyphenation, 177
prepositions, and pronouns, 162–3
prescribed topic, 13

prescribe/proscribe, 195
presentation, in references, 95
presentation, oral, *see* oral presentation
primary material, in planning an essay, 9–10
principle/principal, 195
process explanation, in essay, 24
pronoun reference, 160–1
pronouns: in business reports, 64–5; in lab report, 53;
    and nouns, 160–1; objective, 162–3; possessive,
    168; and prepositions, 162–3; use of, 143, 160–3
publication details, 41, 42
*Publication Manual of the American Psychological
    Association*, 90, 95
publishers, in MLA style, 81
punctuation: apostrophe, 167–8; brackets, 168; colon,
    168–9, 181; comma, 169–74, 180; dash, 174–5; el-
    lipsis, 75, 175–6; en dash, 175; exclamation mark,
    176; hyphen, 176–7; and italics, 74, 75–6, 86, 177–8;
    parentheses, 178–9; period, 179, 180; quotation
    marks, 32, 76, 90, 177–8, 180–1; with quotations,
    32; semicolon, 181–2

qualifiers, 52, 140–1
question marks, indirect questions, 179
questions: in examinations, 120, 121–3, 125–6; in
    introduction, 28–9; in oral presentation, 116–17;
    and periods, 179; in subject analysis, 10
quotation marks: in APA style, 90; in MLA style, 76;
    placement, 180–1; and punctuation, 32; titles of
    works, 177–8, 180
quotations: in APA style, 90; in documenting sources,
    73–5; effective use, 31–2; formatting, 74; guide-
    lines for inclusion, 74–5; in introduction, 28; in
    MLA style, 76–7; and punctuation, 32, 168, 169,
    173, 175; within quotations, 180

race, and bias-free language, 7
rational/rationale, 195
reader: in four Rs and business report, 56–7, 60; think-
    ing about, 2–3
real/really, 195
reason, in four Rs and business report, 55
recommendations, in business report, 60
reference letter, 131
references: in APA style, 93–7; in business report, 63; in
    CSE style, 104, 105, 106; in lab report, 46, 51
references and referees, in resumé, 130–1
relative clauses, 146
repetition, 152
reports, *see* writing a book report; writing a business
    report; writing a lab report
research of topic: in four Rs and business report, 57–8;
    library resources, 16–17; note taking, 18–19; on-
    line sources, 16–18

restricted thesis, 14–15
restrictions, in four Rs and business report, 57
restrictive modifiers, and comma, 172–3
results, in lab report, 46, 49–50
resumé: content, 128–31; preparation and layout, 131–4
revision of essay, 22
roman numeral numbering system, 66
Rs, four, 55–8
run-on sentences, 154–5, 170

's, for possession, 168
saving and backups, 38
scanned book, in MLA style, 89
*Scientific Style and Format: The CSE Manual for
    Authors, Editors, and Publishers*, 104
scientific writing, *see* writing a lab report
seasonable/seasonal, 195–6
secondary sources, 9–10, 73
sections, 59–60, 66–7
semicolon, 181–2
sentences: faulty predication, 156; fragments, 153–4;
    independent clauses, 153–5; and periods, 179;
    structure and length, 150–1; subject in, 142–3;
    unity, 153–6
serial comma, 171
series, 171, 182
she, 6
should of, 196
sic, 74, 168
sight/site/cite, 187
simple sentences, 150–1
site/cite/sight, 187
skimming of material, 9, 40
slang, 3
slashes, in MLA style, 78–9
software, and documentation, 75
sources: acknowledgement, 33–5; in business report,
    58; *see also* documenting sources; electronic
    sources; online sources
special needs, and examinations, 120–1
specificity, 65, 140
speeches, in MLA style, 85
spell checkers, 36–7, 177
spelling, 137–8
squinting modifiers, 163–4
standard resumé, 131–3
style: clarity, 137–45; conciseness, 145–7; and diction,
    137–41; effectiveness, 137; forcefulness, 147–52;
    important ideas in, 149–52; and paragraphs,
    141–5
stylistic flourish, in conclusion, 31
subject (grammatical): and commas, 174; compound,
    157–8; identification, 156–7; in paragraphs, 142–3;
    personal subjects, 148–9

subjectivity, in business reports, 64–5
subject of essay, analysis of, 10–13
subject–verb agreement, 156–8
subordination of ideas, 150
summary: in business report, 59–60; in informative book report, 39–41; in lab report, 46, 47

table of contents, in business report, 63
tables, 49, 66, 69, 72
take/bring, 186
take-home exams, 124
team work, *see* group work
telling fact, in introduction, 29
their/there, 196
theme, *vs.* thesis, 13–14
There is (are)..., 147
thesaurus, 138
thesis: development, 13–16; restriction of, 14–15
they, 7
this, 53, 161
three-C approach, 11–13, 120
title page, 46–7, 62
titles of persons, and commas, 173
titles of works, 158, 177–8, 180
tone, 3–5, 64
topic sentence, in paragraphs, 142
tortuous/torturous, 196
transition words, 144
translator: in Chicago style, 98, 102; in MLA style, 83
translucent/transparent, 196
turbid/turgid, 196

uncertainty values, 49
unified thesis, 15
uninterested/disinterested, 190
unique, 196
URLs, in MLA style, 87
usage: common errors, 153–66; in English language, 138–9; of punctuation, 167–82

values, and uncertainty, 49
verbs: active *vs.* passive, 147–8; agreement with subject, 156–8; and commas, 174; in lab report, 52–3; and modifiers, 163; tenses, 49, 158–60
verse, in MLA style, 78–9
video blogs, in APA style, 97

visual aids, *see* illustrations
volume of a book, in MLA style, 83

we, in business reports, 64
Web magazine, in MLA style, 88
websites: in Chicago style, 100, 103; in CSE style, 108; evaluation of information, 17–18; in MLA style, 87, 88, 89; URLs, 87; *see also* online sources
well/good, 191
while, 196–7
wikis, 18
-wise, 197
word-processing software, and documentation, 75
words: division with hyphens, 176–7; in strategic position, 149; usage and meaning, 138–9
work, finding, *see* letter of application; resumé
works cited, MLA style, 75, 81–90
would of, 188
writer's block, 22
writing: in examinations, 122–3; guidelines, 5; and language, 5–7; purpose of, 2; and the reader, 2–3; strategies, 1–5; and style, 137–52; thinking about, 1–7
writing a book report: analytic book report, 42–4; informative book report, 39–41; introduction of, 42; kinds of, 39; literary review, 44
writing a business report: group reports, 58–9; guidelines, 64–7; important information in, 54, 59–60; organization of information and details, 59–61; parts and sections, 59–60, 62–3; planning, 55–63; principles and purpose, 54–5; sources and accuracy, 58
writing a lab report: calculations in, 49; format and sections, 46–51; graphs and tables, 49–50; overview, 45; purpose and reader of, 45–6, 47; tense and voice in, 49; writing style and advice, 51–3
writing an essay: conclusions, 29–31; editing stage, 35–7; first draft, 22; formatting, 37–8; ideas development, 22–7; introductions, 27–9; organizational patterns, 22–7; outline creation, 19–22; plagiarism, 32–5; planning stage, 8–22; quotations in, 31–2; research of topic, 16–19; saving and backups, 38; subject analysis, 10–11; thesis development, 13–16; writing stage, 22–35
writing examinations, *see* examinations

your/you're, 197

The Making Sense Series

Margot Northey with Joan McKibbin
MAKING SENSE
A Student's Guide to Research and Writing
Eighth Edition

Margot Northey, Dianne Draper, and David B. Knight
MAKING SENSE IN GEOGRAPHY AND ENVIRONMENTAL SCIENCES
A Student's Guide to Research and Writing
Sixth Edition

Margot Northey, Lorne Tepperman, and Patrizia Albanese
MAKING SENSE IN THE SOCIAL SCIENCES
A Student's Guide to Research and Writing
Sixth Edition

Margot Northey and Judi Jewinski
MAKING SENSE IN ENGINEERING AND THE TECHNICAL SCIENCES
A Student's Guide to Research and Writing
Fourth Edition

Margot Northey and Patrick von Aderkas
MAKING SENSE IN THE LIFE SCIENCES
A Student's Guide to Research and Writing
Second Edition

Margot Northey, Bradford A. Anderson, and Joel N. Lohr
MAKING SENSE IN RELIGIOUS STUDIES
A Student's Guide to Research and Writing
Second Edition

Margot Northey and Brian Timney
MAKING SENSE IN PSYCHOLOGY
A Student's Guide to Research and Writing
Second Edition